The Wonders Inside
THE HUMAN BODY

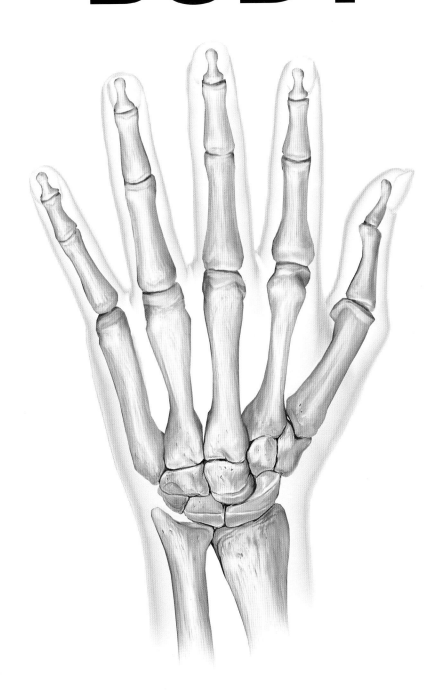

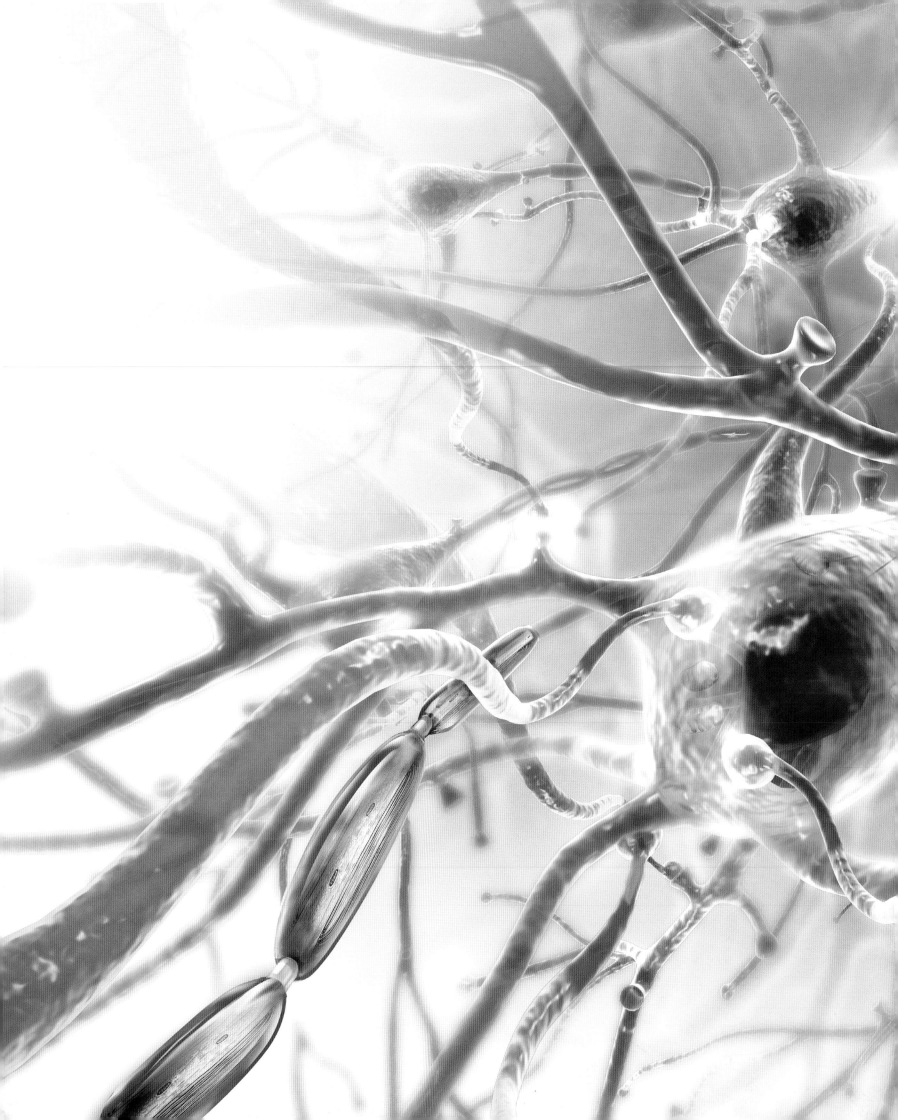

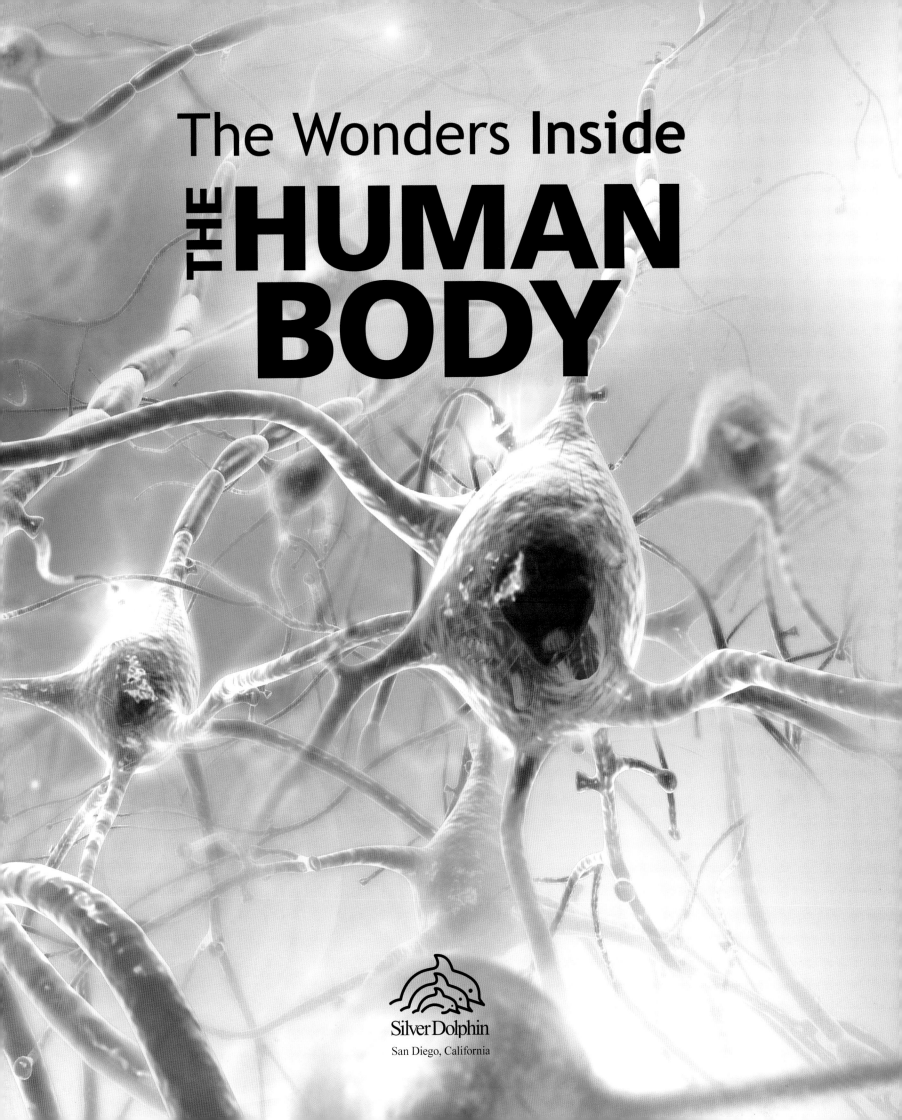

The Wonders Inside

THE HUMAN BODY

Silver Dolphin

San Diego, California

Silver Dolphin Books
An imprint of the Advantage Publishers Group
10350 Barnes Canyon Road, San Diego, CA 92121
www.silverdolphinbooks.com

Conceived and produced by Weldon Owen Pty Ltd
59–61 Victoria Street, McMahons Point
Sydney NSW 2060, Australia

Copyright © 2009 Weldon Owen Pty Ltd
First published 2009

ISBN-13: 978-1-57145-718-9
ISBN-10: 1-57145-718-6

Color reproduction by Chroma Graphics (Overseas) Pte Ltd
Printed by SNP Leefung Printers Ltd
Manufactured in China
1 2 3 4 5   13 12 11 10 09

A WELDON OWEN PRODUCTION

BONNIER BOOKS
Group Publisher John Owen

WELDON OWEN PTY LTD
Chief Executive Officer Sheena Coupe
Creative Director Sue Burk
Publisher Margaret Whiskin
Senior Vice President, International Sales Stuart Laurence
Vice President, Sales: United States and Canada Amy Kaneko
Vice President, Sales: Asia and Latin America Dawn Low
Administration Manager, International Sales Kristine Ravn
Production Manager Todd Rechner
Production Coordinators Lisa Conway, Mike Crowton

Project Editor Erin O'Brien
Author Jan Stradling
Consultant Dr. Robin Arnold
Cover Design Sarah Norton
Designer Sarah Norton
Art Manager Trucie Henderson
Illustrations Argosy Publishing

ARGOSY PUBLISHING
Director, Medical Art Bert Oppenheim
Senior Medical Illustrators Joe Gorman, Chris Scalici
Medical Illustrators Kevin Brennan, Maya Chaphalkar, Anne Matuskowitz

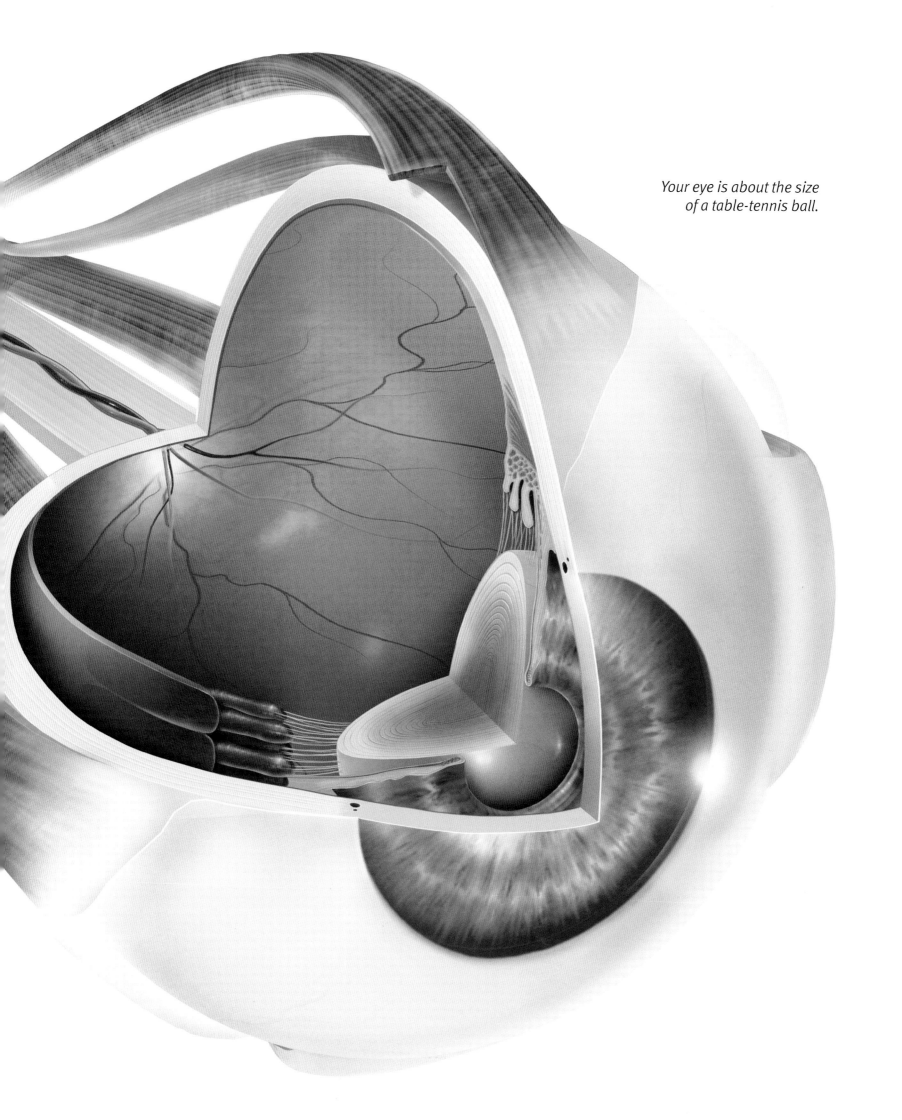

Your eye is about the size of a table-tennis ball.

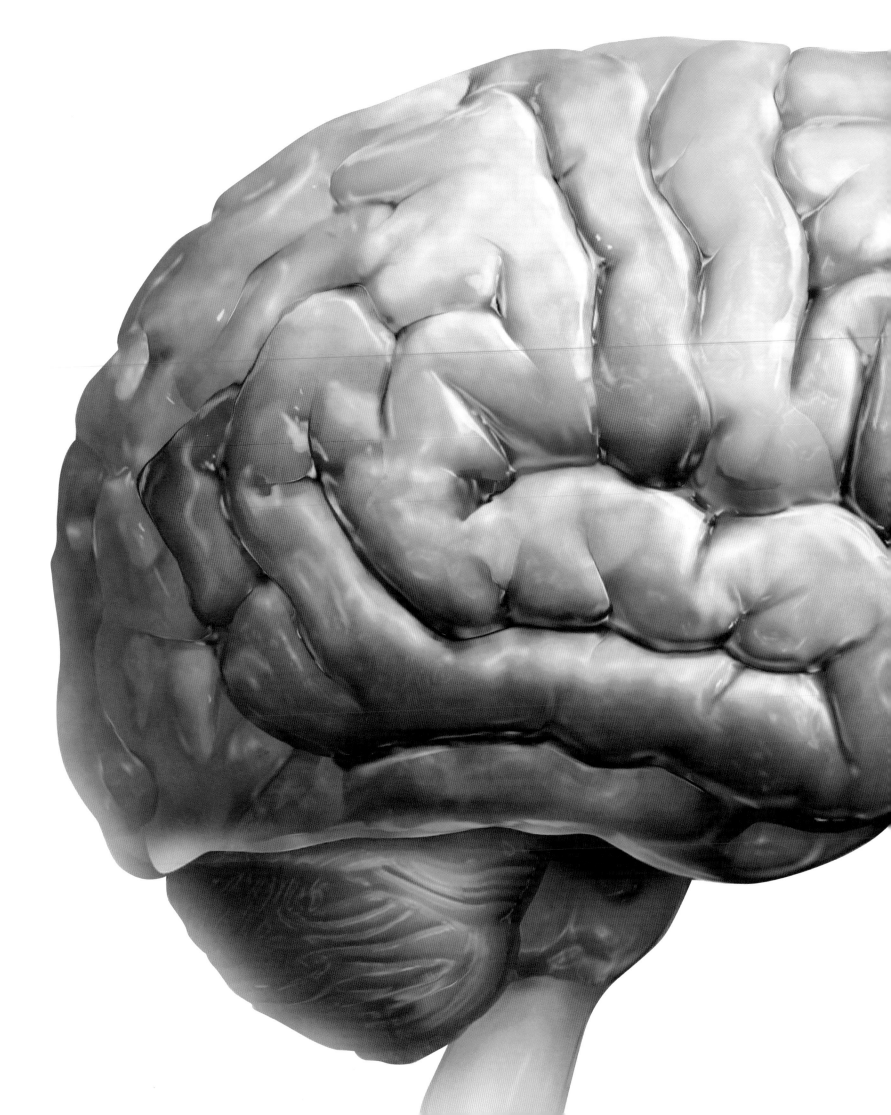

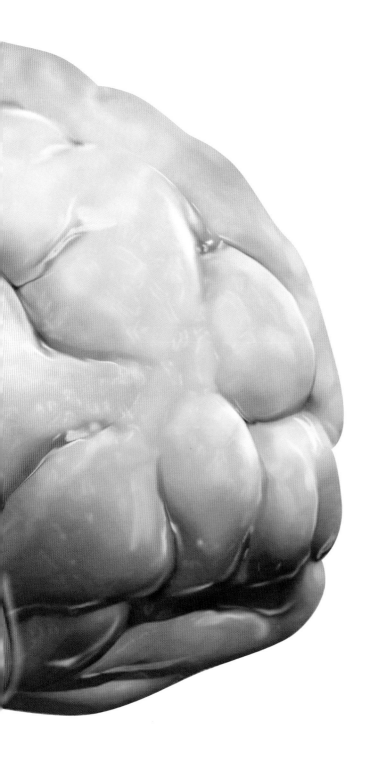

CONTENTS

The Basics Head to Toe Senses Systems Layers

THE BODY

Your body is like a machine. It has many different parts that work together so you can function properly. Adults have 26 billion brain cells, 650 muscles, 206 bones, 100,000 miles of blood vessels, and many other parts that keep the body working. Organs, such as the heart and stomach, do special jobs and work with other parts of your body to form systems—and your brain is in charge of the whole machine. Billions of cells, hundreds of muscles and bones, and thousands of miles of blood vessels are just some of the parts inside your body that keep you alive.

Brain *The control center that tells your body what to do.*

Lung *Your body has two spongy organs called lungs. They take oxygen out of the air and send carbon dioxide out of the body.*

Heart *The heart pumps blood full of oxygen around the body.*

Stomach *Juices in the stomach help break down the food you eat.*

Small intestine *Starts to digest your food.*

Large intestine *More digestion happens here.*

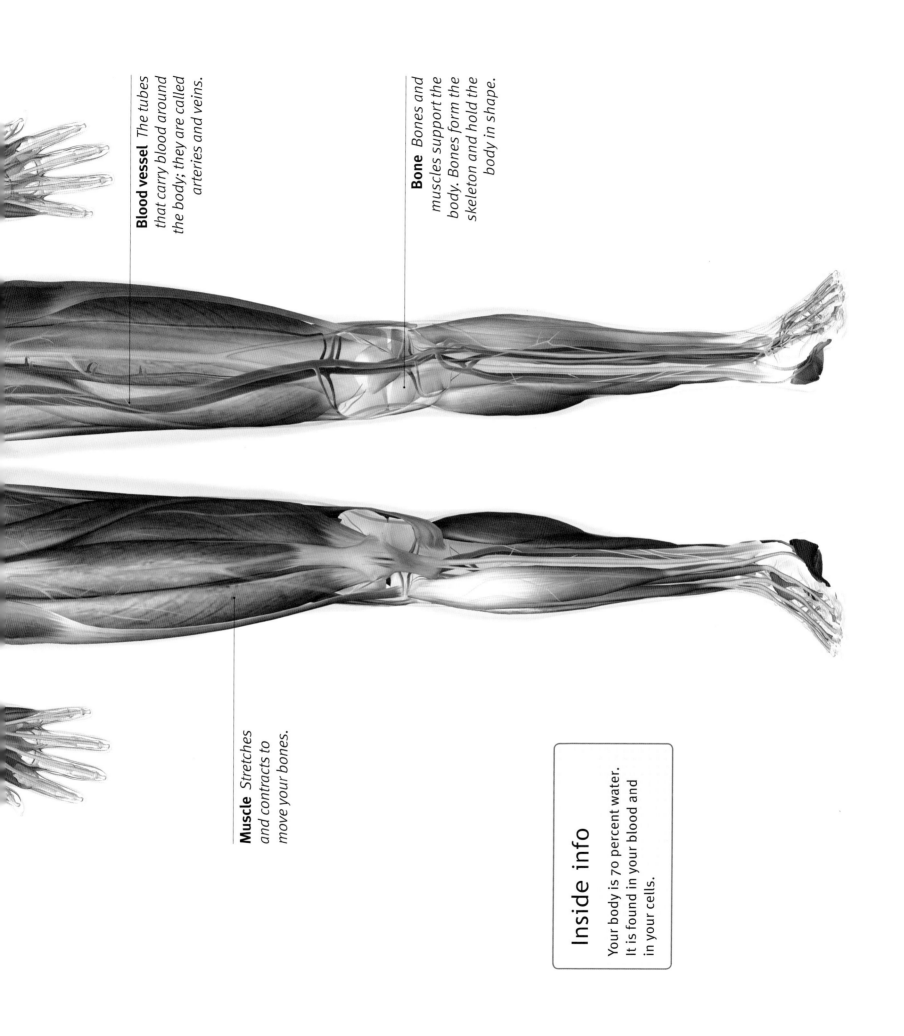

Blood vessel *The tubes that carry blood around the body; they are called arteries and veins.*

Bone *Bones and muscles support the body. Bones form the skeleton and hold the body in shape.*

Muscle *Stretches and contracts to move your bones.*

Inside info

Your body is 70 percent water. It is found in your blood and in your cells.

CELLS

Cells are the building blocks that make up almost all living things. Cells are protected by an outer cover called a membrane, which lets in good things, such as nutrients, and keeps out bad things, such as bacteria. Most cells have a nucleus in the middle, which instructs the cell what to do. You have more than 200 kinds of cells in your body, and they all have different jobs.

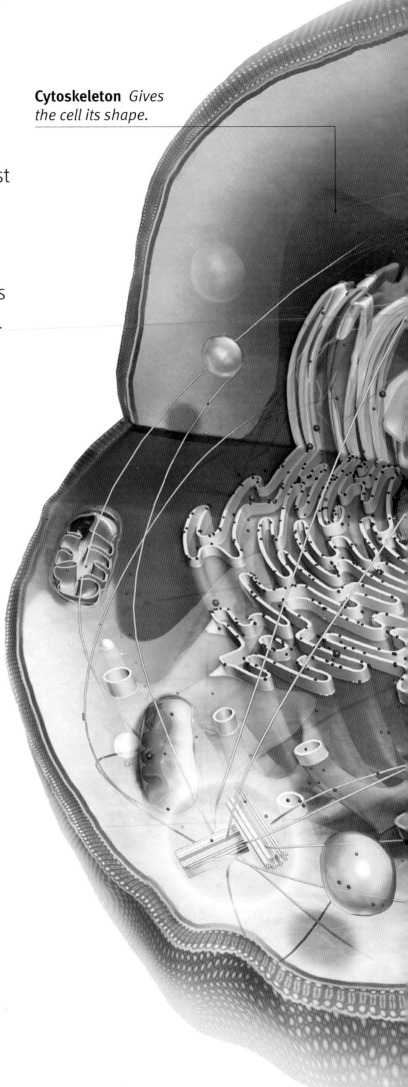

Cytoskeleton *Gives the cell its shape.*

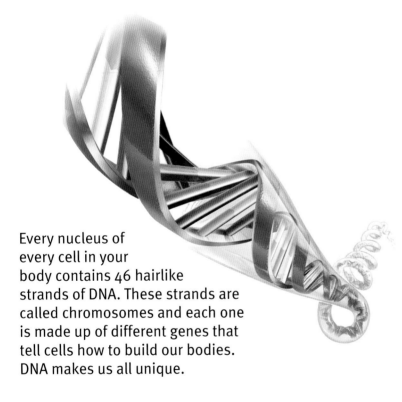

Every nucleus of every cell in your body contains 46 hairlike strands of DNA. These strands are called chromosomes and each one is made up of different genes that tell cells how to build our bodies. DNA makes us all unique.

Inside info

Your body contains about 100 million million tiny cells. By the time you have finished reading this sentence, 50 million of your cells will have died and been replaced!

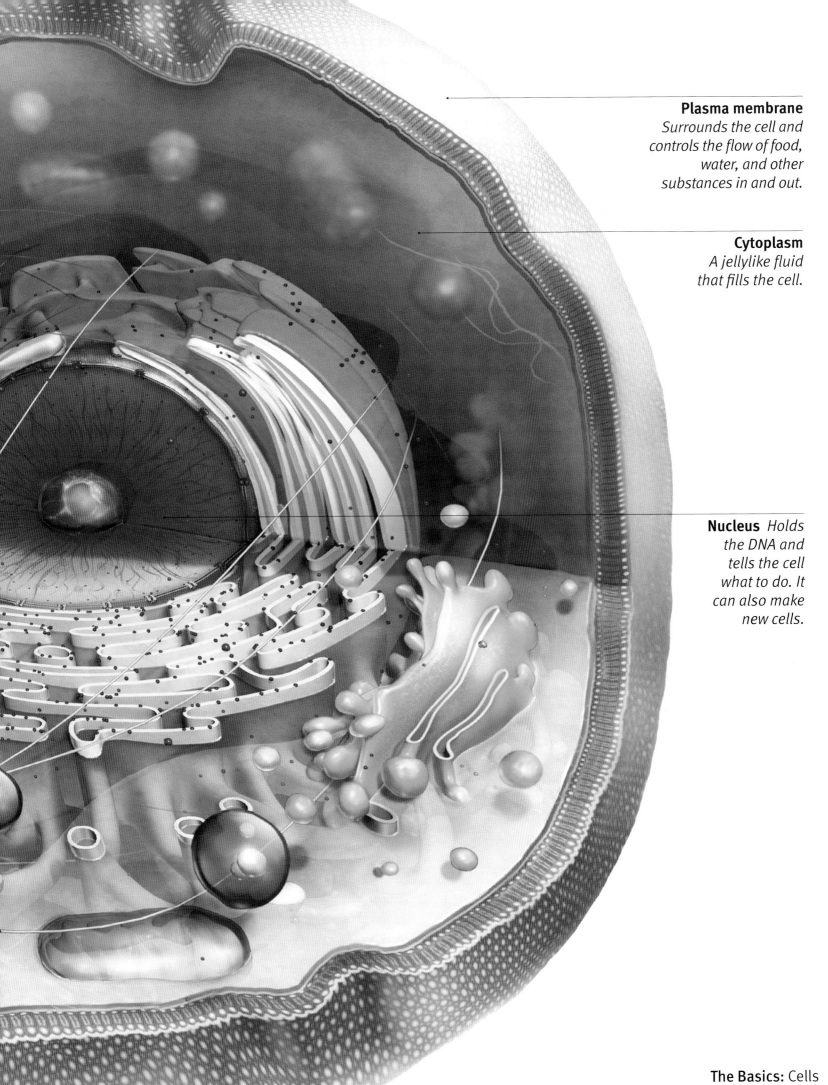

Plasma membrane
Surrounds the cell and controls the flow of food, water, and other substances in and out.

Cytoplasm
A jellylike fluid that fills the cell.

Nucleus *Holds the DNA and tells the cell what to do. It can also make new cells.*

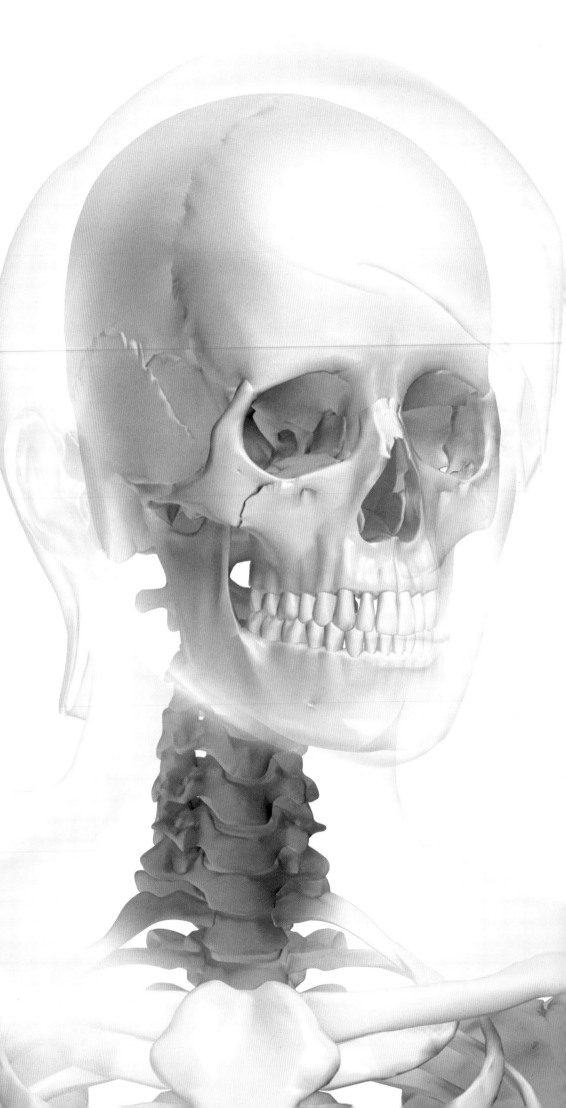

THE HEAD

Page 12 *The skull is made up of 29 bones that protect the brain and support the face and neck muscles.*

Page 13 *This is a view of the brain, eyes, nerves, and blood vessels, without their muscles. Veins are shown in blue, arteries in red, and nerves in yellow.*

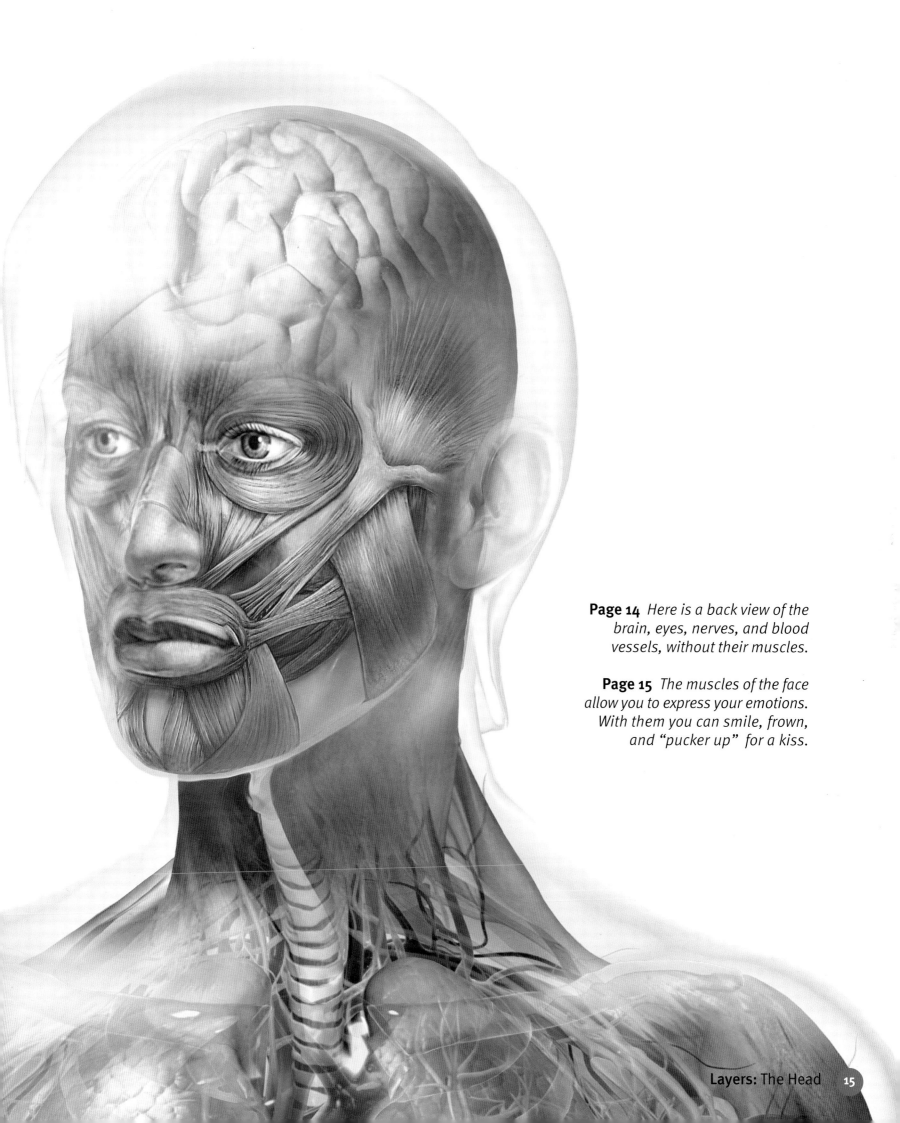

Page 14 *Here is a back view of the brain, eyes, nerves, and blood vessels, without their muscles.*

Page 15 *The muscles of the face allow you to express your emotions. With them you can smile, frown, and "pucker up" for a kiss.*

TISSUE REPAIR

There are four types of body tissues. Each consists of groups of cells that all have different jobs to do. Epithelial tissue covers organs and makes up the skin. Connective tissue holds body organs in place. Muscle tissue helps you move, and nervous tissue carries signals from the brain to the rest of the body. When tissue is damaged, your body begins to repair itself right away.

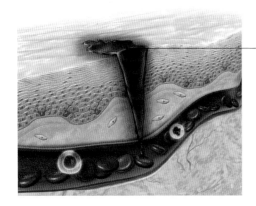

Inflammation

When you cut yourself, your body acts quickly. The area around the cut becomes red and swells. Infection-fighting cells then make a clot to stop the bleeding.

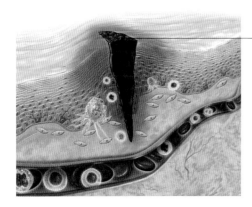

Blood clot

New blood vessels enter and fill the wound. Cells form collagen, a type of protein. It connects and supports tissues such as skin, bone, and muscles, which helps the tissue recover.

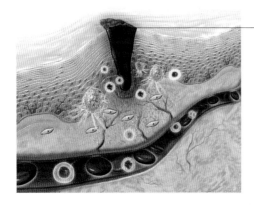

Scab

The collagen starts to make another layer of new tissue. A scab forms on the open wound and the new tissue starts to fill the injured area.

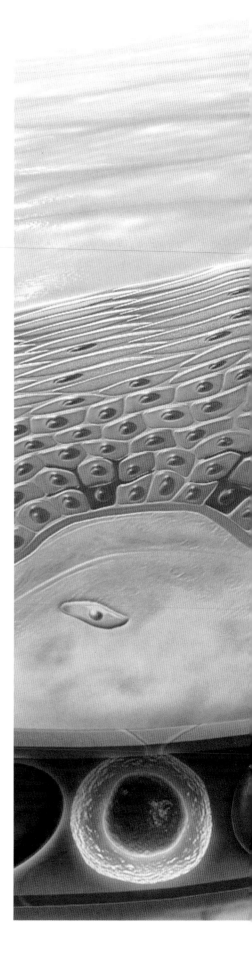

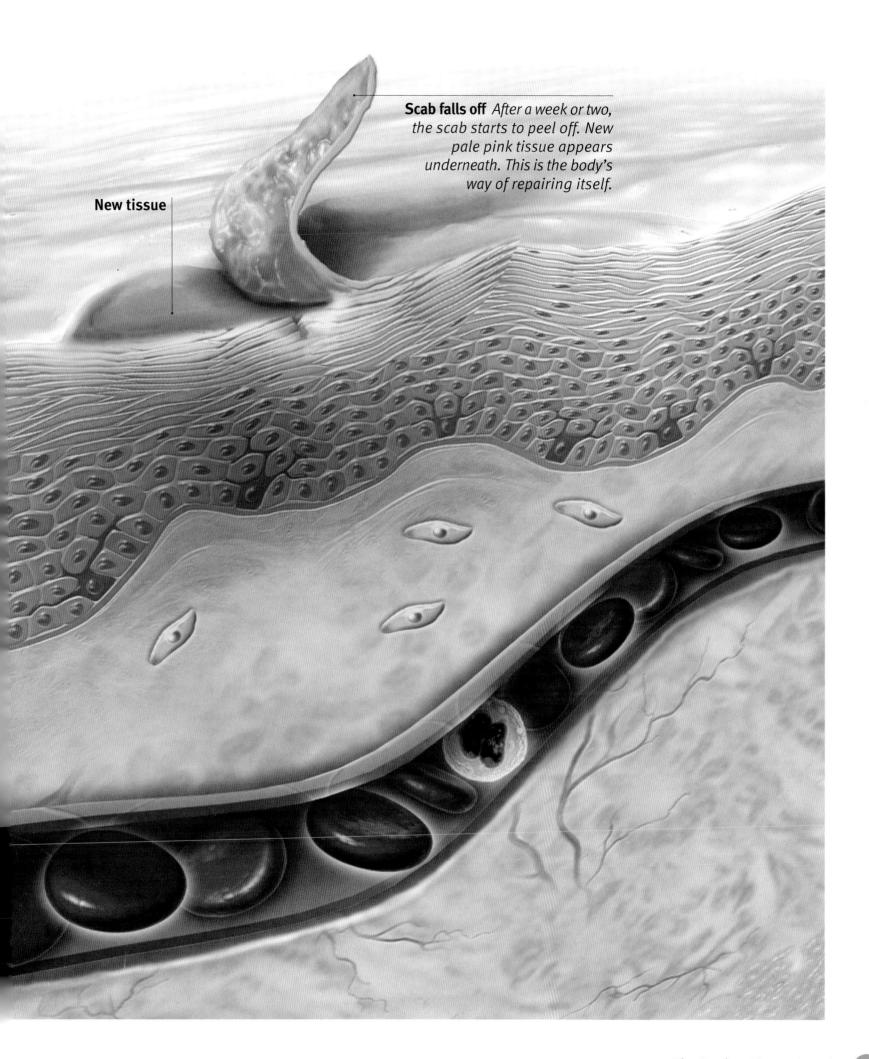

New tissue

Scab falls off *After a week or two, the scab starts to peel off. New pale pink tissue appears underneath. This is the body's way of repairing itself.*

SKIN

Skin is your largest and heaviest organ. An adult's skin weighs about 11 pounds and covers almost 22 square feet, which is the size of a single bed. Skin holds your body together and keeps water, germs, and dirt from getting in. The dermis, the inner layer, provides strength and support to your skin. Below this is a layer of fat that keeps your body temperature steady.

Nerve *Nerve endings send messages to your brain.*

Sweat gland *Makes sweat that travels out onto your skin to cool you down.*

Hair follicle

Muscle

Goosebump

Each hair is attached to a muscle cell below the skin's surface. When you are cold or scared, the muscle cell contracts and makes the hair stand on end. This makes a little bump, which we call a "goosebump."

Artery

Vein

Epidermis *The outer layer of skin is several cells thick.*

Dermal papilla *Brings blood close to the surface of the skin so it can easily absorb nutrients.*

HAIR

Hair, skin, fingernails, and toenails are all made from a protein called keratin. Hair grows everywhere on your body except on the palms of your hands, the soles of your feet, and your lips. The outer layer of your nails, hair, and skin is dead, but under the skin new cells are constantly being made. Your skin is covered in special glands that oil your skin and hair, which keeps them soft.

Free edge

Nail plate

Nail root

Your nail has three main parts: the nail plate is the part you can see, the nail root at the base of the nail is where keratin is made, and the free edge is at the tip.

Hair shaft

Hair root

Nerve ending

Bulb

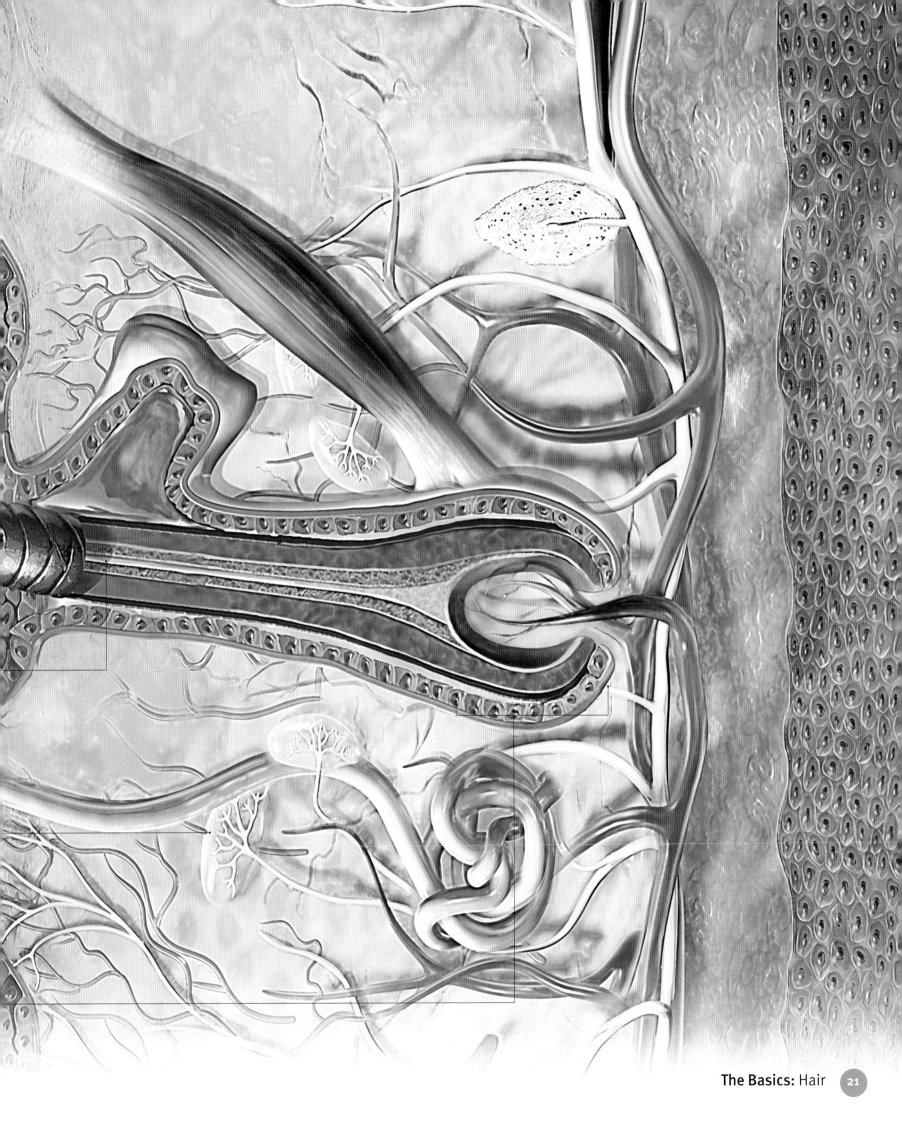

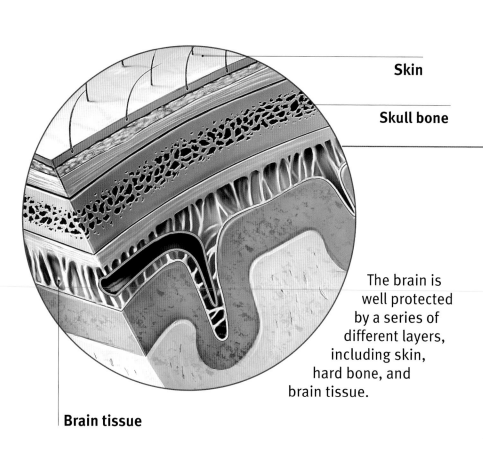

Skin

Skull bone

The brain is well protected by a series of different layers, including skin, hard bone, and brain tissue.

Brain tissue

THE BRAIN

Your brain is your control center. It processes the information from incoming nerve signals so that you know what you see, smell, and taste, as well as whether you are hot, hungry, or in pain. The brain also sends outgoing signals that control your body's activities, such as when you sweat during exercise. Memories, feelings, and imagination are all functions of the billions of cells that make up your brain.

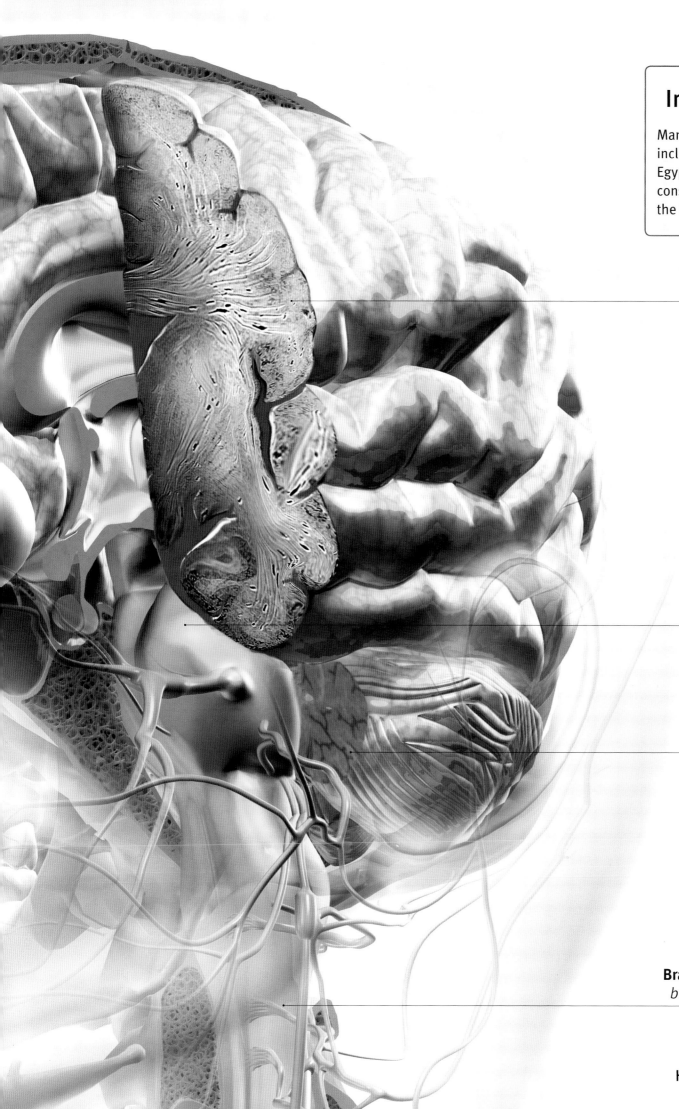

Inside info

Many ancient cultures, including the Greeks and Egyptians, believed that consciousness resided in the heart, not in the brain.

Cerebral cortex *This outer layer is, at the most, one-sixth of an inch thick, but tens of millions of cells communicate here every moment of your life.*

Medulla oblongata *Controls the body's involuntary functions, such as breathing and digestion.*

Cerebellum *Helps you maintain balance and keeps your movements smooth.*

Brain stem *Connects your brain to your spinal cord.*

EMOTION

A ring of small structures in your brain allows you to feel emotions, such as anger, happiness, and love. As this area starts to sense an emotion, the prefrontal cortex helps you decide what to do with your feelings. When a toddler has a tantrum, it is a sign that the prefrontal cortex is still growing and the toddler is not yet able to control feelings. Emotions play a large part in memory—you are much more likely to remember how to do something you enjoy than something you do not like doing.

People cannot read minds, but we do get "hunches," or gut feelings. Scientists suspect this is because our brains remember experiences and emotions we think we have forgotten.

Prefrontal cortex
Helps you use judgment and reason to control your emotions.

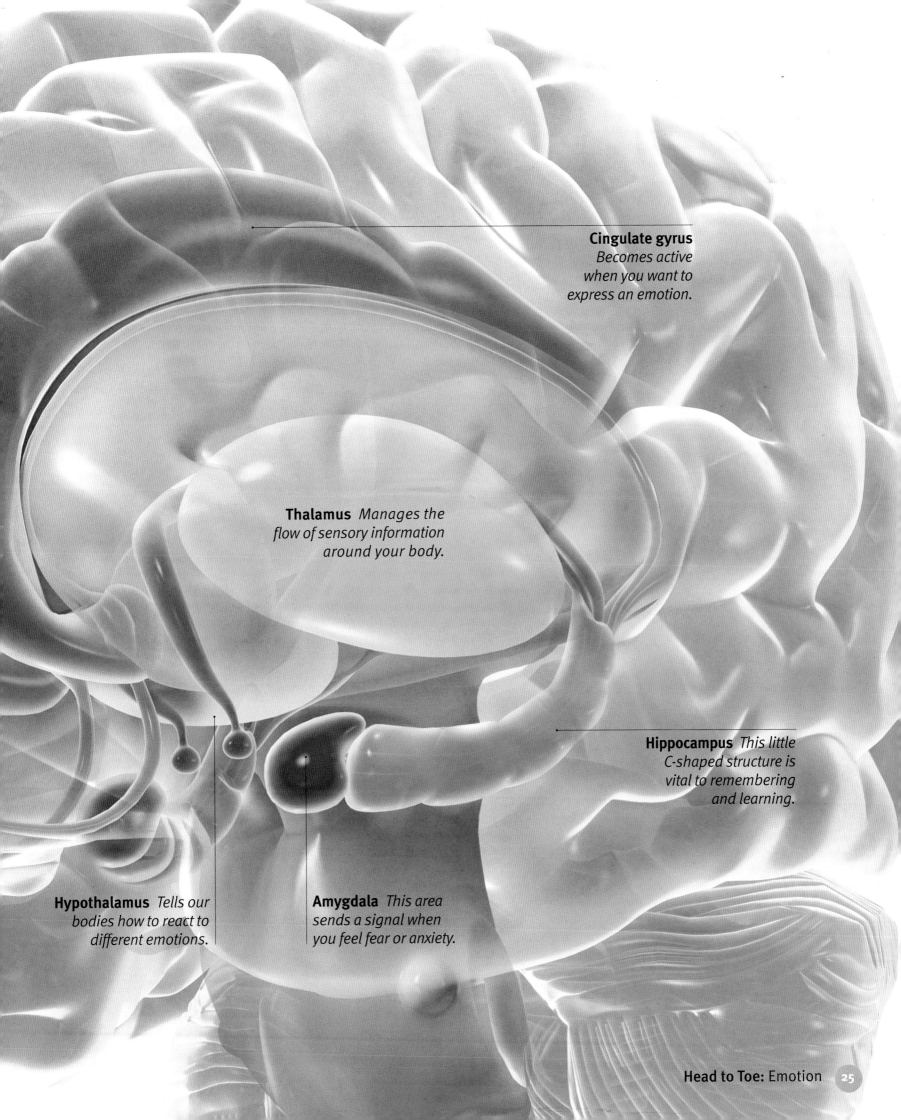

Cingulate gyrus *Becomes active when you want to express an emotion.*

Thalamus *Manages the flow of sensory information around your body.*

Hippocampus *This little C-shaped structure is vital to remembering and learning.*

Hypothalamus *Tells our bodies how to react to different emotions.*

Amygdala *This area sends a signal when you feel fear or anxiety.*

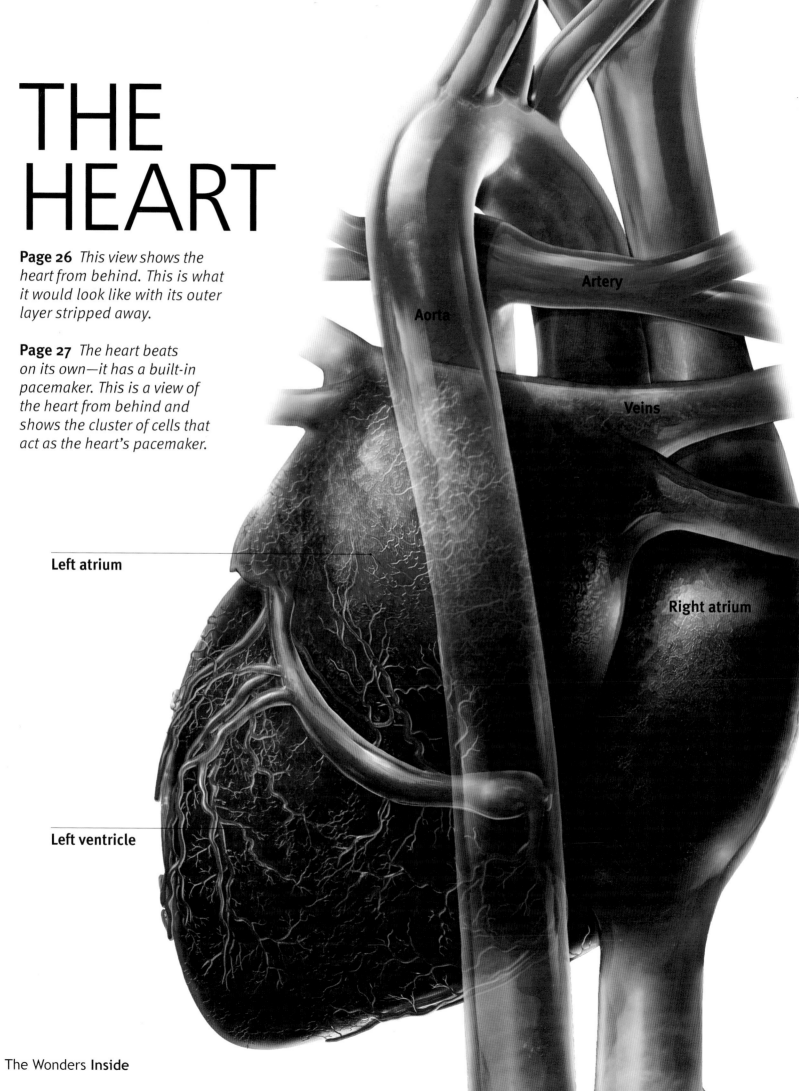

THE HEART

Page 26 *This view shows the heart from behind. This is what it would look like with its outer layer stripped away.*

Page 27 *The heart beats on its own—it has a built-in pacemaker. This is a view of the heart from behind and shows the cluster of cells that act as the heart's pacemaker.*

Aorta

Artery

Veins

Right atrium

Left atrium

Left ventricle

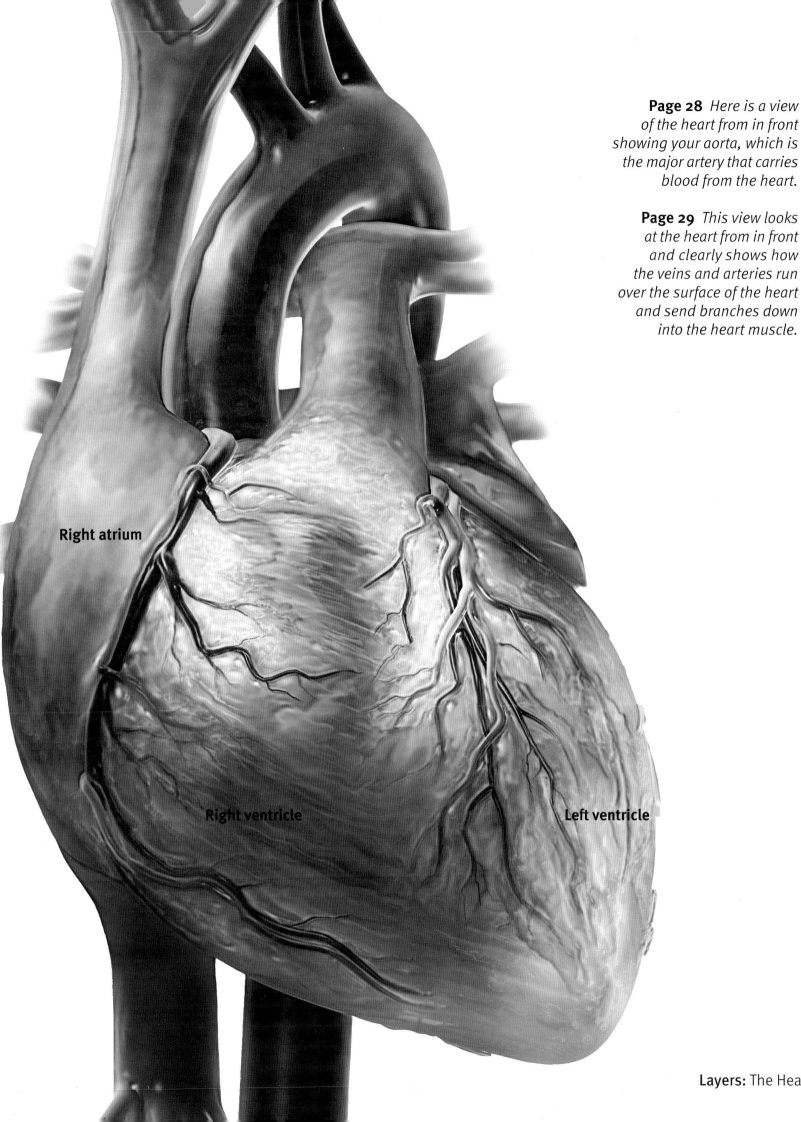

Aorta

Right atrium

Right ventricle

Left ventricle

Page 28 *Here is a view of the heart from in front showing your aorta, which is the major artery that carries blood from the heart.*

Page 29 *This view looks at the heart from in front and clearly shows how the veins and arteries run over the surface of the heart and send branches down into the heart muscle.*

CARDIAC CYCLE

Your heart beats about 100,000 times each day. With each heartbeat, your heart contracts, or squeezes, and then relaxes. The four chambers of your heart form two pumps. The right ventricle pumps blood from the body to the lungs. The left ventricle pumps oxygen-rich blood from the lungs to the body. Your heart pumps blood around your body 24 hours a day.

Into your heart *Your heart has four main parts: a left and right atrium at the top, and a left and right ventricle below. Blood from the body flows into the right atrium. Blood from the lungs flows into the left atrium.*

Left atrium fills with blood

Right atrium fills with blood

Left ventricle

Right ventricle

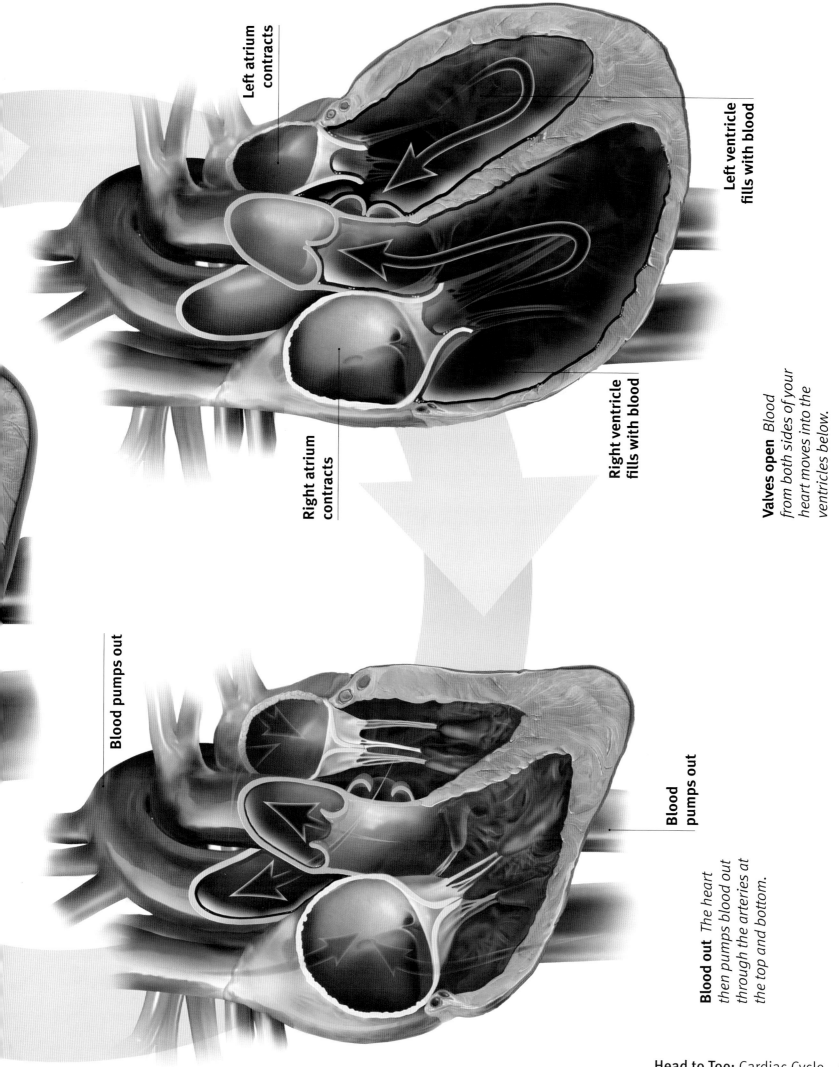

Left atrium contracts

Left ventricle fills with blood

Right atrium contracts

Right ventricle fills with blood

Valves open *Blood from both sides of your heart moves into the ventricles below.*

Blood pumps out

Blood pumps out

Blood out *The heart then pumps blood out through the arteries at the top and bottom.*

ARMS

The bones, joints, and muscles that make up your arms and hands allow you to do lots of different things, such as play the piano, throw a ball, or paint a picture. Your arm consists of three long bones. The bone of your upper arm is connected to your lower arm at your elbow joint. The structure of the elbow joint allows you to turn your hand and forearm upside down.

Inside info

Your "funny bone" is not a bone at all. It is a nerve that runs down the inside of your elbow. It may get its name because it is near the humerus bone of your upper arm.

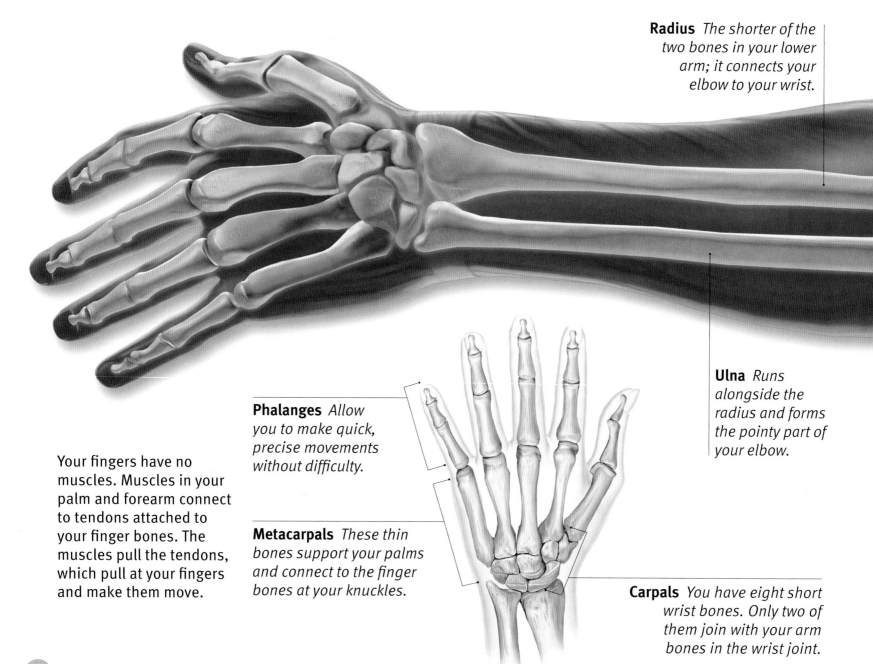

Radius *The shorter of the two bones in your lower arm; it connects your elbow to your wrist.*

Ulna *Runs alongside the radius and forms the pointy part of your elbow.*

Your fingers have no muscles. Muscles in your palm and forearm connect to tendons attached to your finger bones. The muscles pull the tendons, which pull at your fingers and make them move.

Phalanges *Allow you to make quick, precise movements without difficulty.*

Metacarpals *These thin bones support your palms and connect to the finger bones at your knuckles.*

Carpals *You have eight short wrist bones. Only two of them join with your arm bones in the wrist joint.*

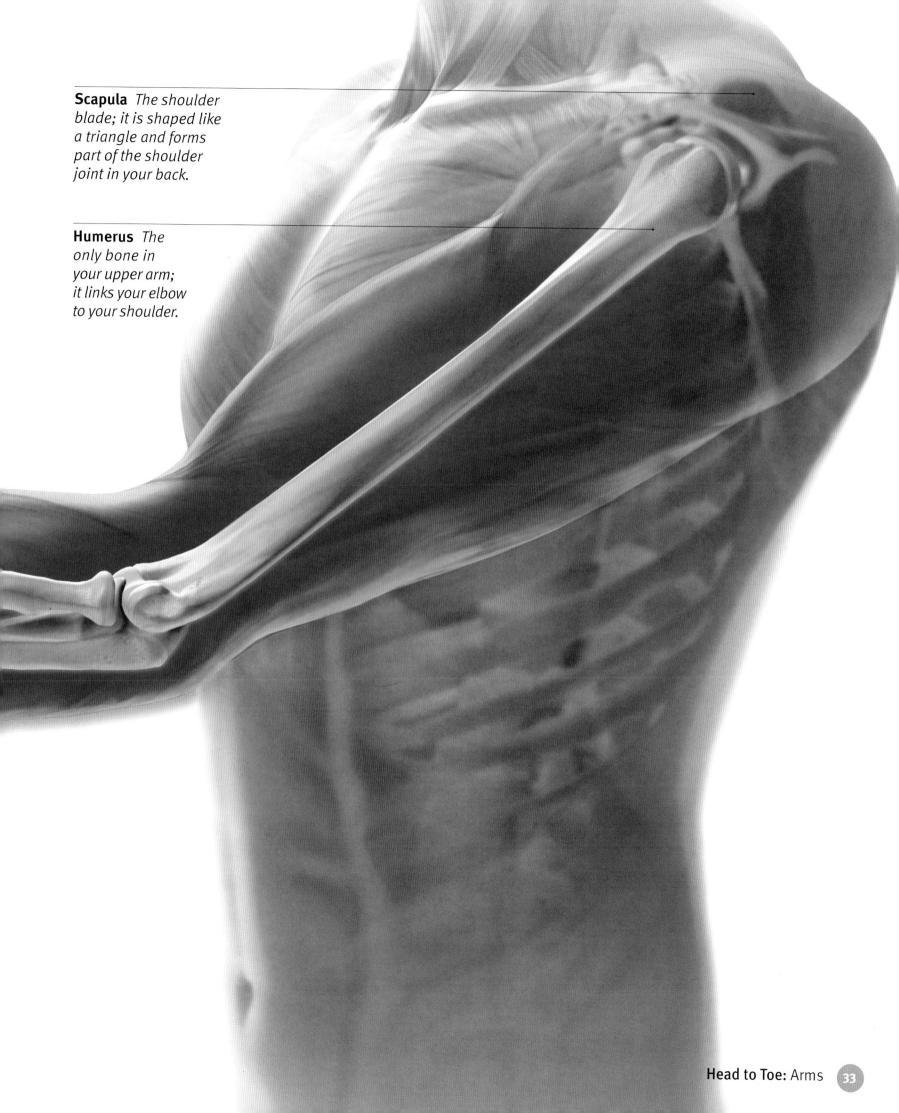

Scapula *The shoulder blade; it is shaped like a triangle and forms part of the shoulder joint in your back.*

Humerus *The only bone in your upper arm; it links your elbow to your shoulder.*

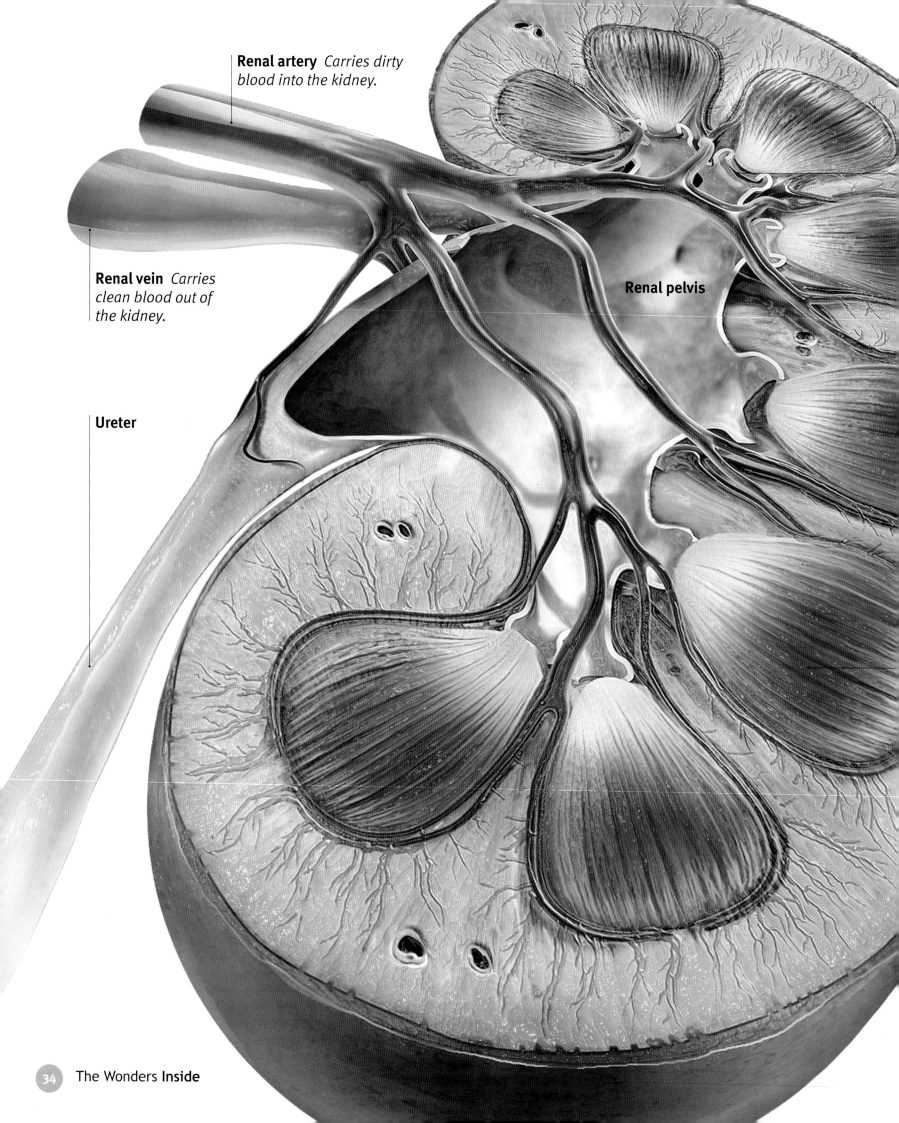

Renal artery *Carries dirty blood into the kidney.*

Renal vein *Carries clean blood out of the kidney.*

Ureter

Renal pelvis

Calyx *Urine flows from the calyx to the renal pelvis and to the ureter.*

KIDNEYS

Kidneys take the waste out of your blood. Each kidney has about a million tiny filtering units called nephrons. They work together to clean your blood and make sure your body has the right levels of water, salt, and other substances. Once your blood is clean, it is returned to the bloodstream. Extra water, salt, and a waste product called urea become urine. Urine travels from your kidneys to your bladder in two tubes called ureters. Urine is stored in your bladder until it is released through another tube called a urethra.

Renal cortex *Cleans the blood through special filters.*

Renal medulla *Helps clean blood to reabsorb water.*

Males and females have the same urinary systems except for the urethra. In males, this channel is about 9 inches long. The female urethra is only about 2 inches long.

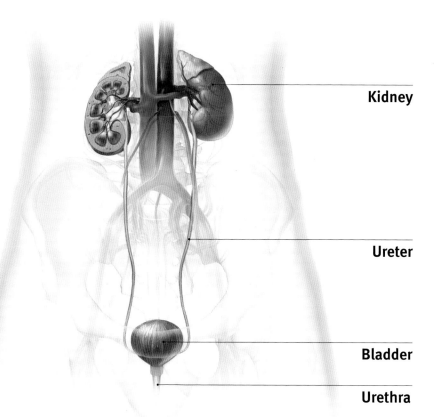

Kidney

Ureter

Bladder

Urethra

THE CHEST

Page 36 *The muscles of the chest help the body push, throw, and climb. The major chest muscle is called the pectoralis major.*

Page 37 *Ribs form a wall that protects the internal organs, such as the lungs and the liver.*

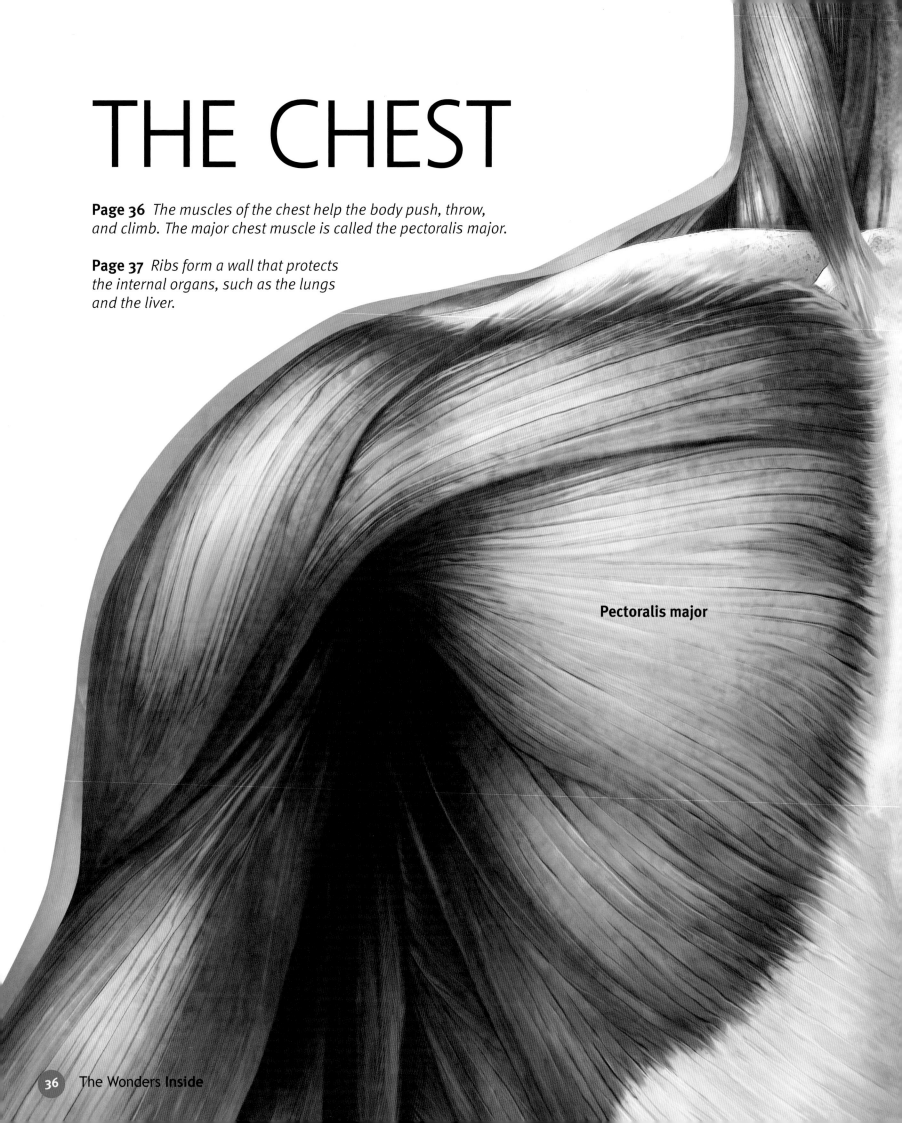

Pectoralis major

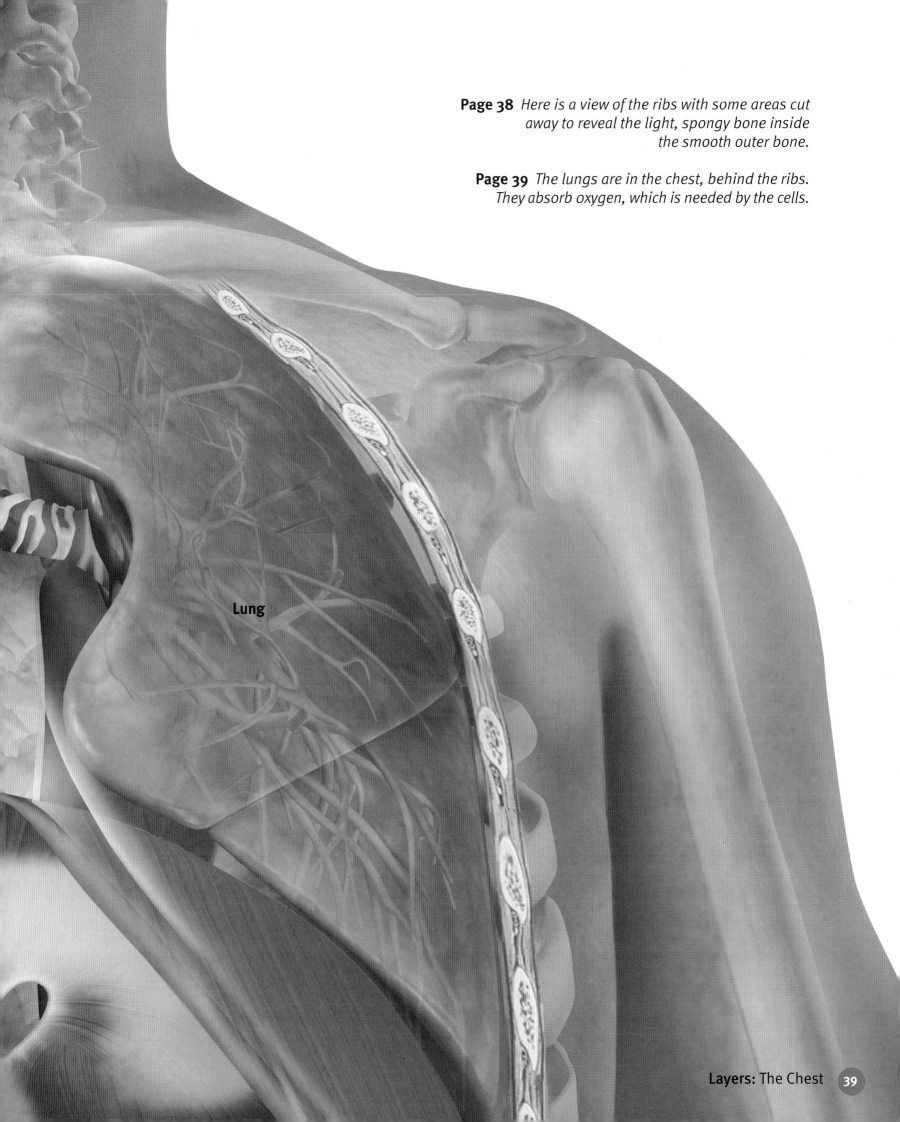

Page 38 *Here is a view of the ribs with some areas cut away to reveal the light, spongy bone inside the smooth outer bone.*

Page 39 *The lungs are in the chest, behind the ribs. They absorb oxygen, which is needed by the cells.*

Lung

REPRODUCTION

A baby begins as one tiny cell. This cell divides in two and doubles in size, and the baby gets bigger. By the end of three months, the baby is nearly 6 inches long and all of its body organs are formed. The central nervous system soon starts to communicate with the muscles and the baby begins to move. By the ninth month, all of the baby's body systems are developed. Throughout these months, the baby is connected to its mother by an umbilical cord. This cord carries blood, oxygen, and nutrients to the baby from the placenta.

Inside info

A baby has no fingerprints when it is born. It takes three months for them to develop.

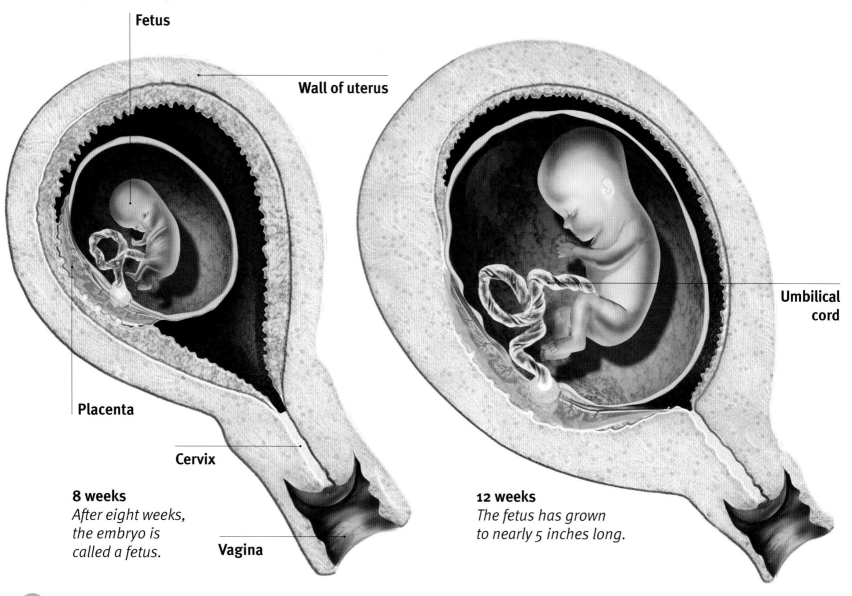

Fetus

Wall of uterus

Umbilical cord

Placenta

Cervix

8 weeks
After eight weeks, the embryo is called a fetus.

Vagina

12 weeks
The fetus has grown to nearly 5 inches long.

When you reach puberty, your body changes. Both males and females grow body hair. A female gains breasts and she becomes more curved around the stomach and hips. The male gets more muscles and his voice deepens.

Breasts

Muscles

Curves

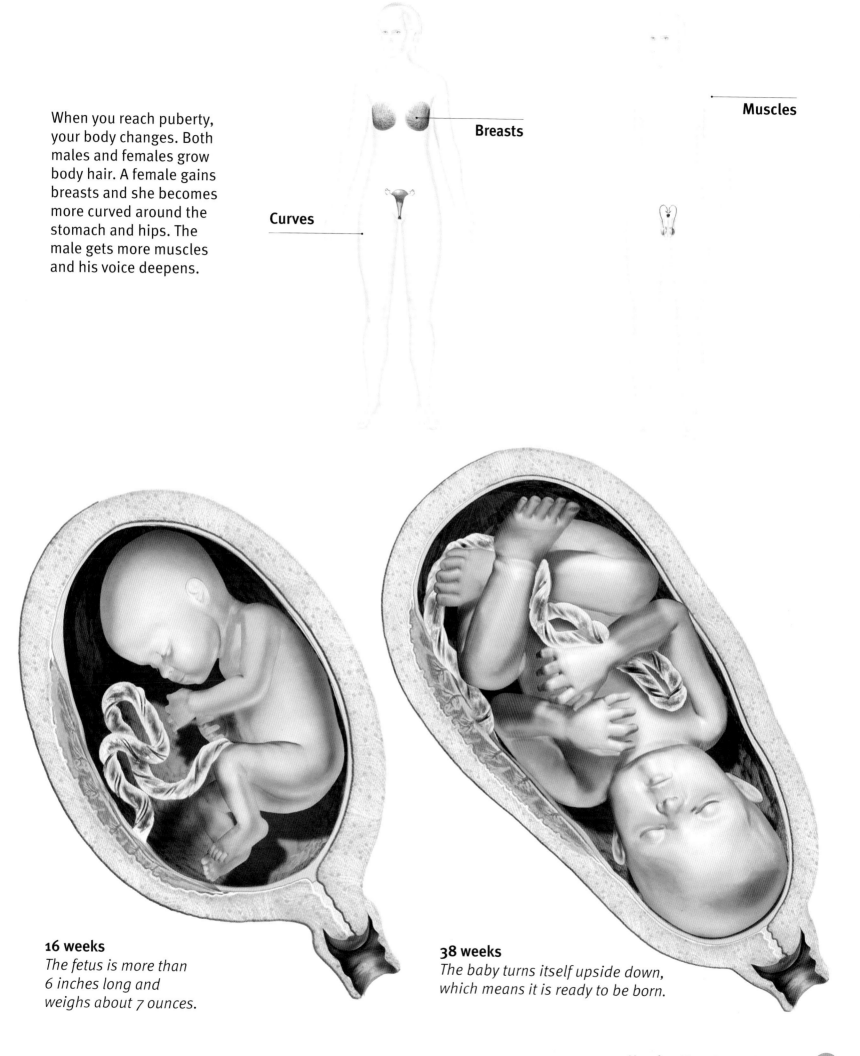

16 weeks
The fetus is more than 6 inches long and weighs about 7 ounces.

38 weeks
The baby turns itself upside down, which means it is ready to be born.

LEGS

Bones in your legs and feet work together so that you can walk and balance. Most of your bones are fully formed by the time you are 12 years old, but your arms and legs keep growing until you are about 20 years old. Bones, muscles, and tendons in your legs have to be strong to hold your body. Your legs are made up of four bones: the femur (thighbone), the patella (kneecap), the tibia, and the fibula.

Inside info

The length of your thighbone is about a quarter of your height, no matter what age you are.

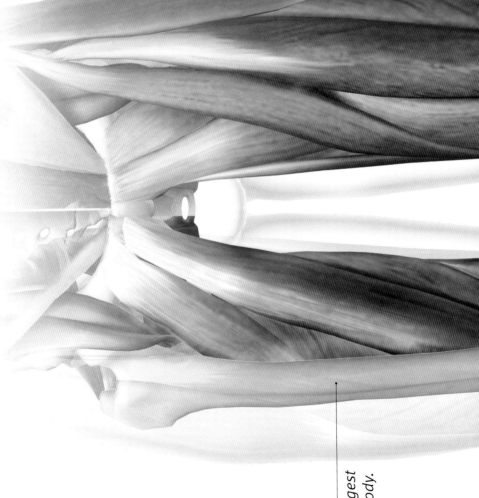

Femur *The longest bone in your body.*

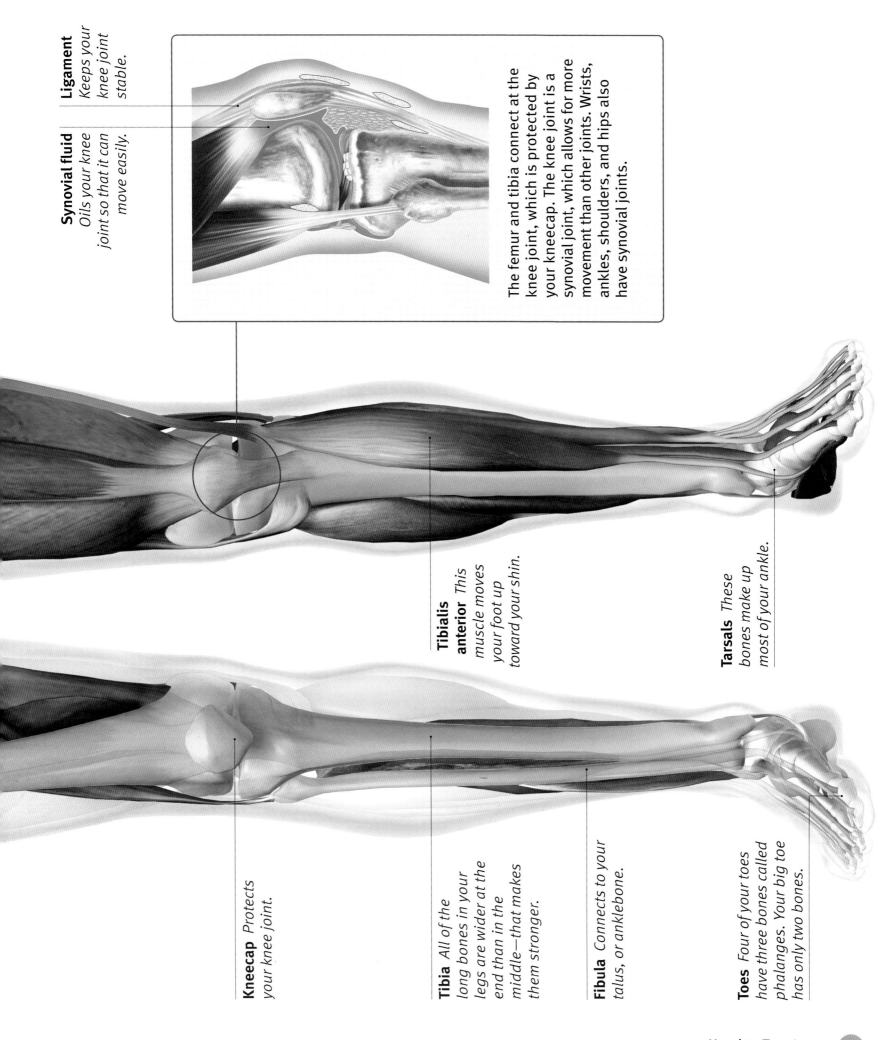

Ligament *Keeps your knee joint stable.*

Synovial fluid *Oils your knee joint so that it can move easily.*

The femur and tibia connect at the knee joint, which is protected by your kneecap. The knee joint is a synovial joint, which allows for more movement than other joints. Wrists, ankles, shoulders, and hips also have synovial joints.

Tibialis anterior *This muscle moves your foot up toward your shin.*

Tarsals *These bones make up most of your ankle.*

Kneecap *Protects your knee joint.*

Tibia *All of the long bones in your legs are wider at the end than in the middle—that makes them stronger.*

Fibula *Connects to your talus, or anklebone.*

Toes *Four of your toes have three bones called phalanges. Your big toe has only two bones.*

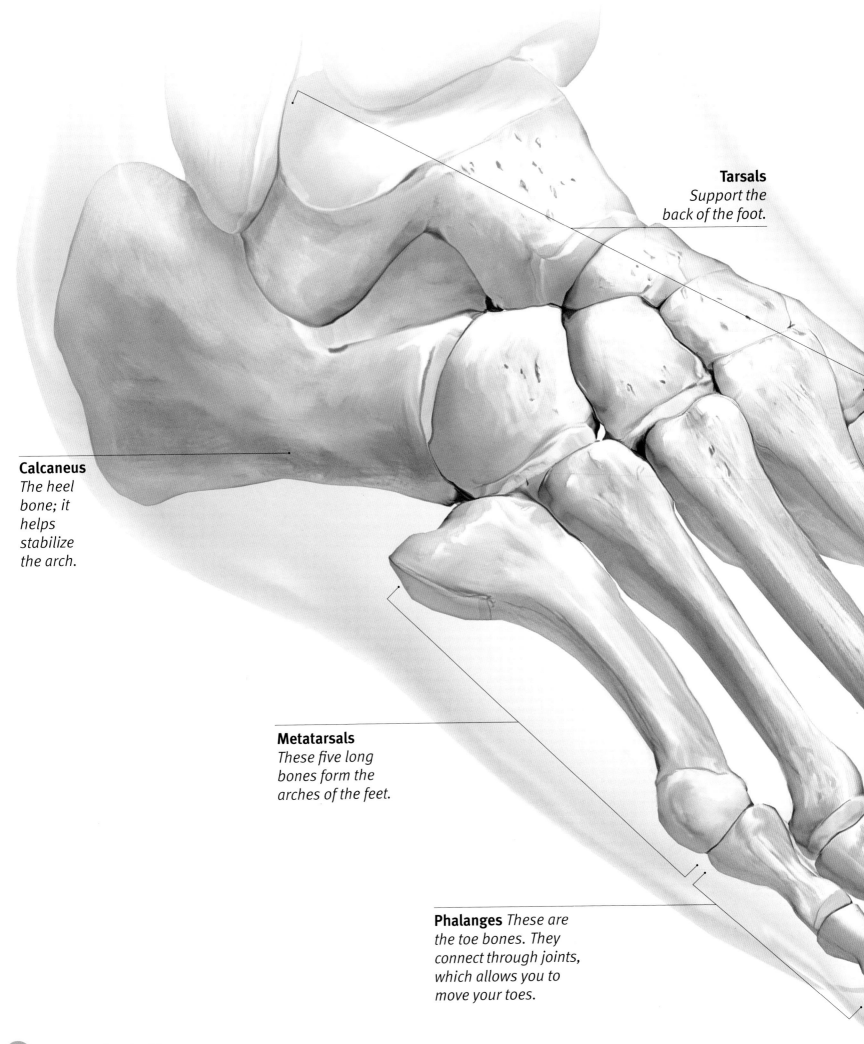

Tarsals
Support the back of the foot.

Calcaneus
The heel bone; it helps stabilize the arch.

Metatarsals
These five long bones form the arches of the feet.

Phalanges *These are the toe bones. They connect through joints, which allows you to move your toes.*

FEET

Your "hanging skeleton" contains the bones of limbs that help you move, such as your hands and feet. Your feet support the weight of your body and also help you balance. Each foot has 26 bones, 33 joints, and 19 muscles, which work together to make sure your feet can be flexible and strong. One quarter of all of the bones in your body are found in your feet.

The bones in your feet form arches that help carry your weight. When a person has flat feet, it means that the tendons have weakened and the arch has fallen.

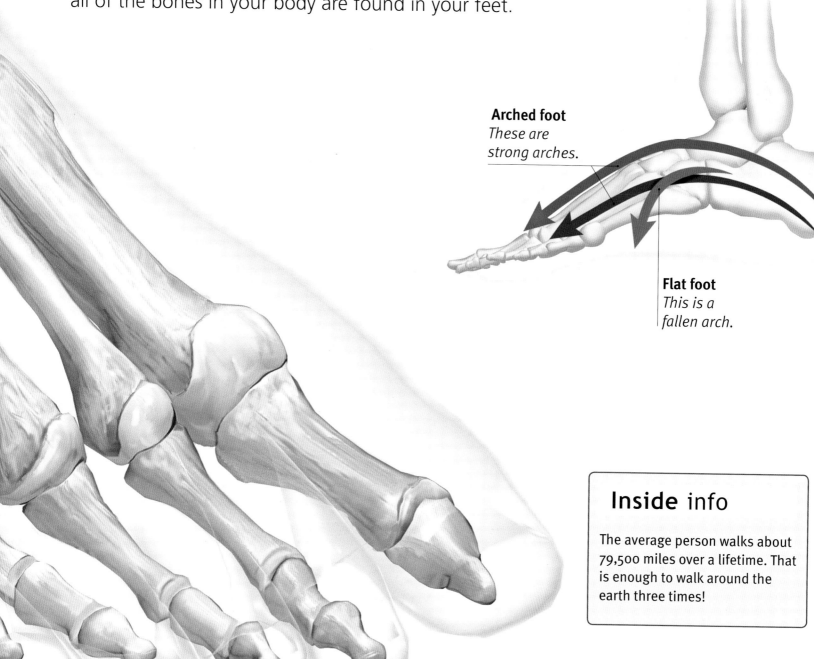

Arched foot
These are strong arches.

Flat foot
This is a fallen arch.

Inside info

The average person walks about 79,500 miles over a lifetime. That is enough to walk around the earth three times!

SENSES

You depend on millions of sensory receptors that tell you what is happening inside and outside your body. General senses feel temperature, touch, pressure, and pain, while special senses control vision, hearing, smell, taste, and balance. When sensory receptors detect something, they send messages to your central nervous system. This system is in charge of everything your body does and feels.

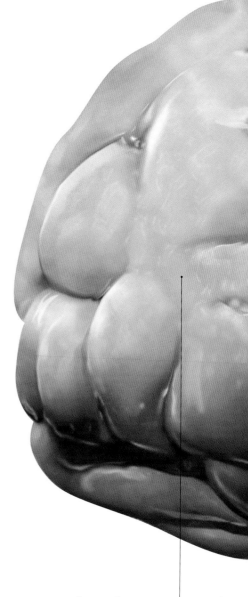

You have 12 pairs of nerves in your brain. Some of these carry information from the sense organs to your brain. Others control muscles, and some connect to organs, such as your heart and lungs.

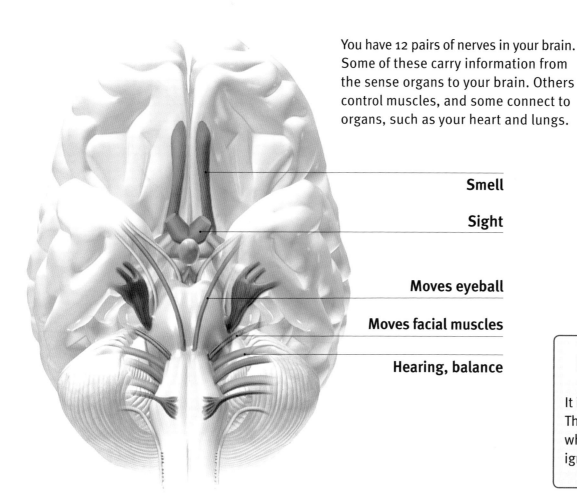

Smell

Sight

Moves eyeball

Moves facial muscles

Hearing, balance

Organizes your thoughts and behavior

Inside info

It is impossible to tickle yourself. This is because your brain knows what you are about to do and ignores the sensation.

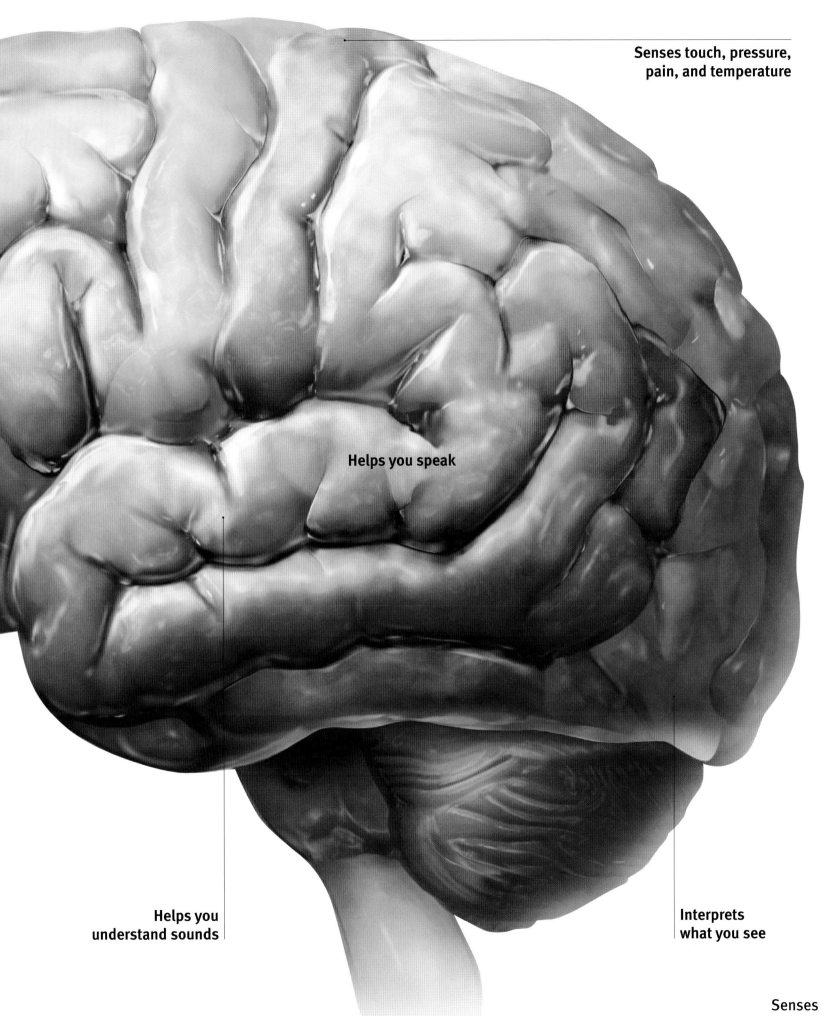

Senses touch, pressure, pain, and temperature

Helps you speak

Helps you understand sounds

Interprets what you see

TOUCH

Your skin is full of tiny receptors that tell you what you are feeling. As soon as you touch something, the receptors send messages along nerve cells to your brain. Your brain then identifies what the sensation is and where you are feeling it. There are many sensations, such as heat, cold, vibration, pressure, and pain. Different receptors help you feel different sensations.

Sensory receptors for touch are found in your skin's epidermis and the dermis below it. There are about 100 touch receptors in each of your fingertips.

Inside info

The most sensitive areas of your body are your hands, lips, face, neck, tongue, feet, and fingertips.

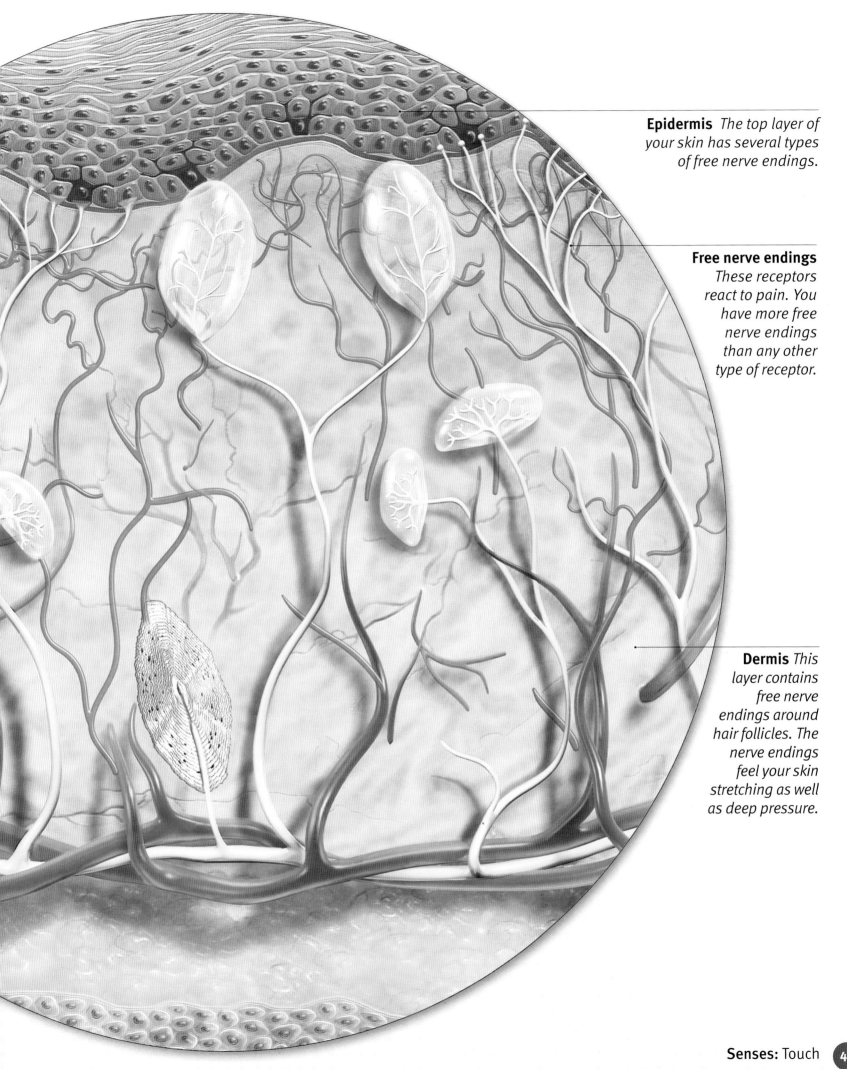

Epidermis *The top layer of your skin has several types of free nerve endings.*

Free nerve endings *These receptors react to pain. You have more free nerve endings than any other type of receptor.*

Dermis *This layer contains free nerve endings around hair follicles. The nerve endings feel your skin stretching as well as deep pressure.*

THE EYE

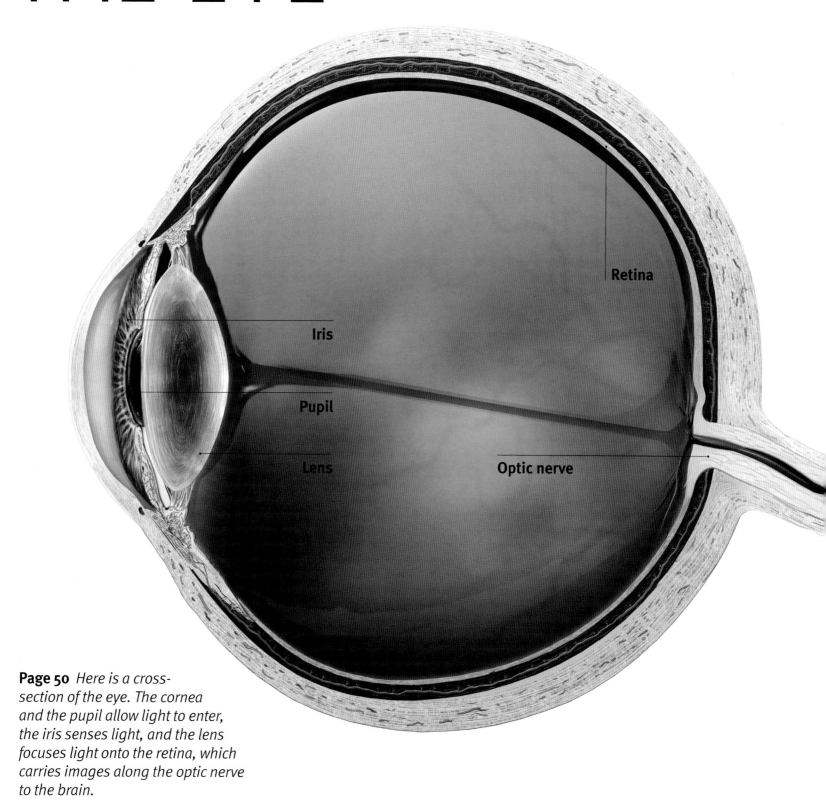

Retina

Iris

Pupil

Lens

Optic nerve

Page 50 *Here is a cross-section of the eye. The cornea and the pupil allow light to enter, the iris senses light, and the lens focuses light onto the retina, which carries images along the optic nerve to the brain.*

Page 51 *The eyeball is surrounded by small muscles that help the eye move. The white of the eye is called the sclera. This protects the eyeball.*

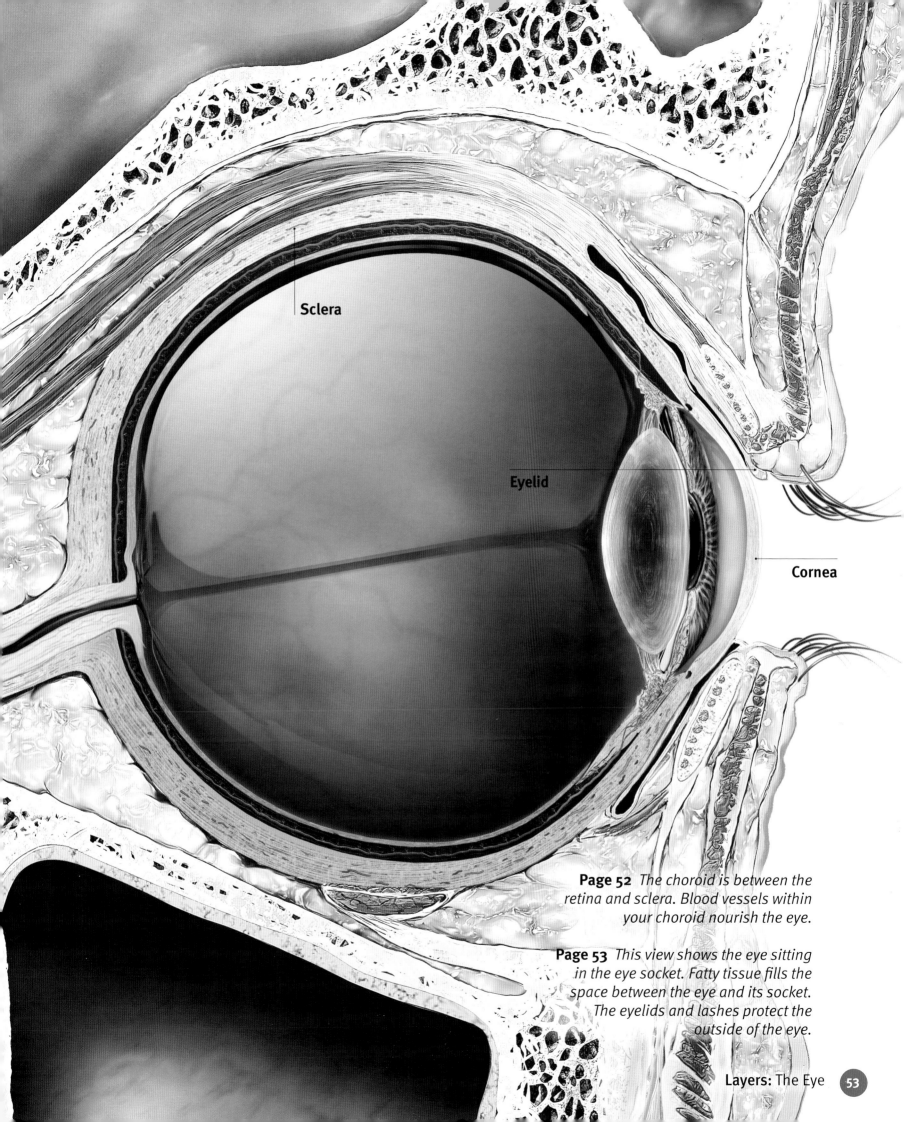

Sclera

Eyelid

Cornea

Page 52 *The choroid is between the retina and sclera. Blood vessels within your choroid nourish the eye.*

Page 53 *This view shows the eye sitting in the eye socket. Fatty tissue fills the space between the eye and its socket. The eyelids and lashes protect the outside of the eye.*

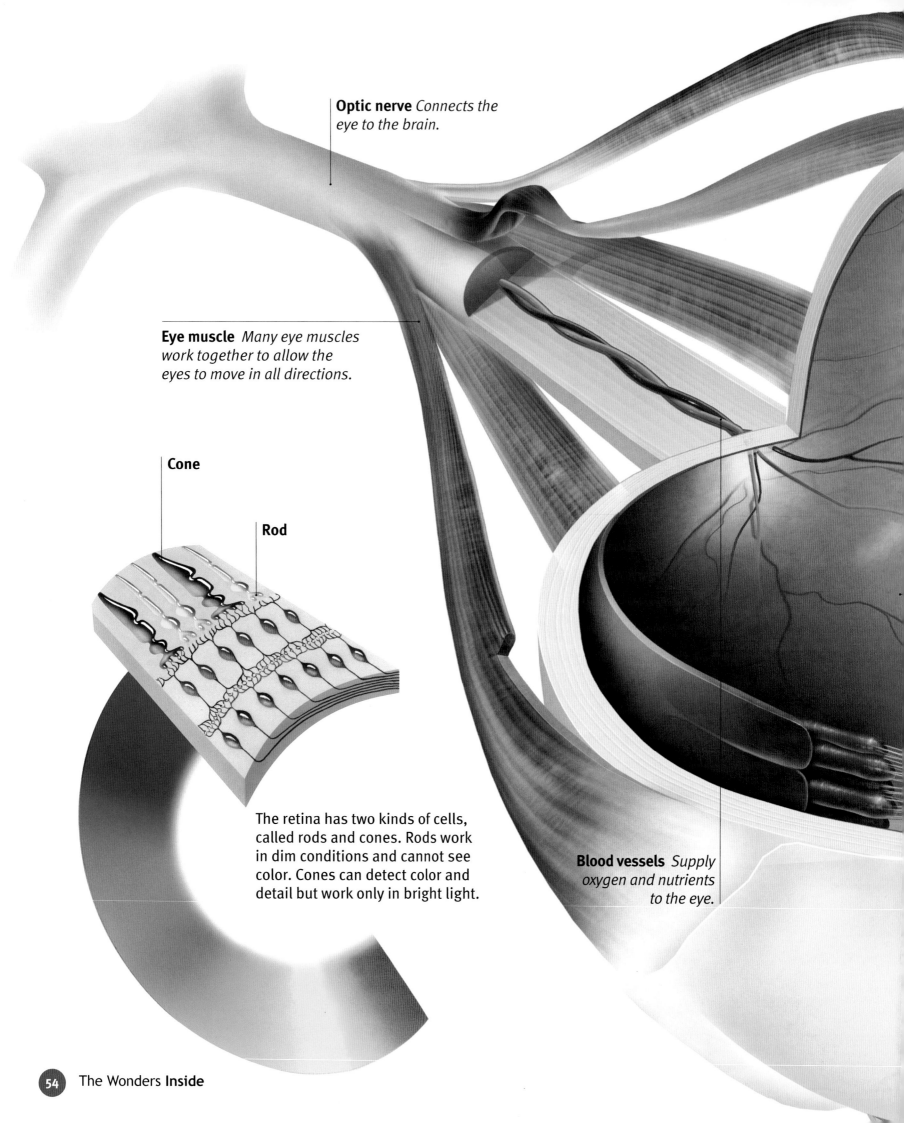

Optic nerve *Connects the eye to the brain.*

Eye muscle *Many eye muscles work together to allow the eyes to move in all directions.*

Cone

Rod

The retina has two kinds of cells, called rods and cones. Rods work in dim conditions and cannot see color. Cones can detect color and detail but work only in bright light.

Blood vessels *Supply oxygen and nutrients to the eye.*

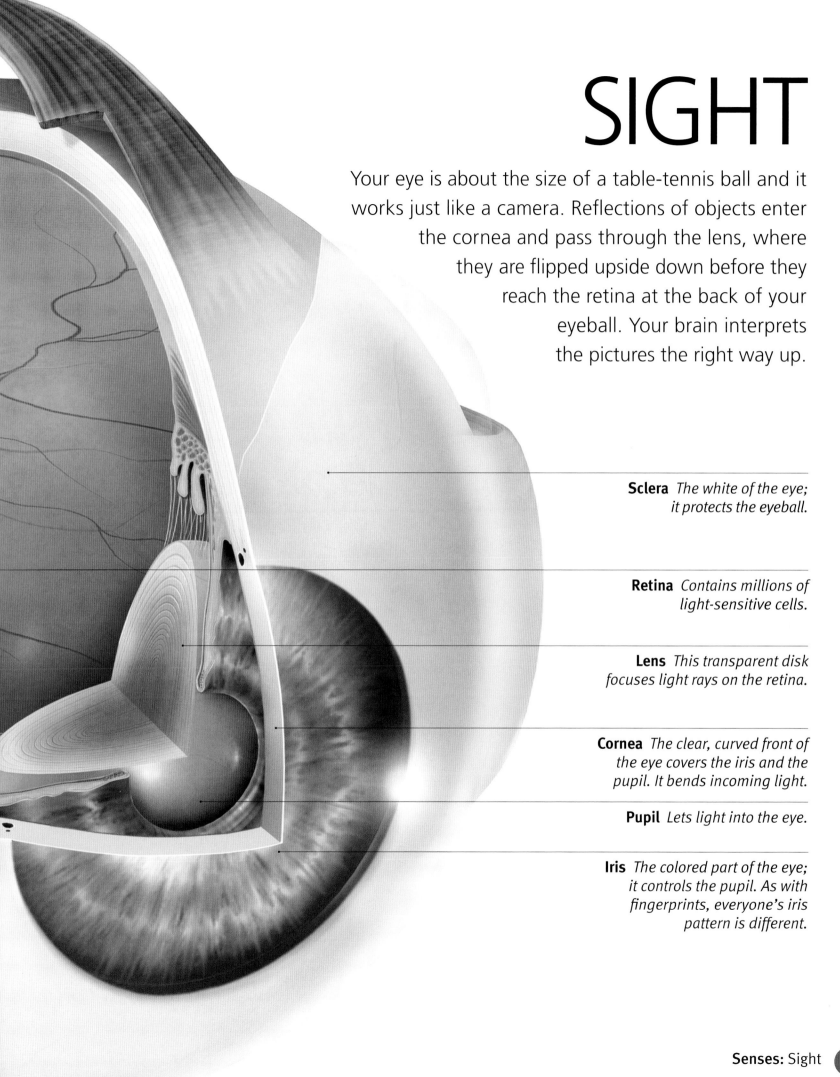

SIGHT

Your eye is about the size of a table-tennis ball and it works just like a camera. Reflections of objects enter the cornea and pass through the lens, where they are flipped upside down before they reach the retina at the back of your eyeball. Your brain interprets the pictures the right way up.

Sclera *The white of the eye; it protects the eyeball.*

Retina *Contains millions of light-sensitive cells.*

Lens *This transparent disk focuses light rays on the retina.*

Cornea *The clear, curved front of the eye covers the iris and the pupil. It bends incoming light.*

Pupil *Lets light into the eye.*

Iris *The colored part of the eye; it controls the pupil. As with fingerprints, everyone's iris pattern is different.*

HEARING

All sounds travel in invisible sound waves. These sound waves move along the ear canal until they hit your eardrum. The eardrum vibrates and causes a ripple effect. The ripple travels along three tiny bones and through the oval window of the cochlea, deep in your ear. Tiny hair cells in the cochlea turn the vibrations into electrical signals that are sent to the brain. Your brain then interprets the electrical signals, allowing you to discern sounds.

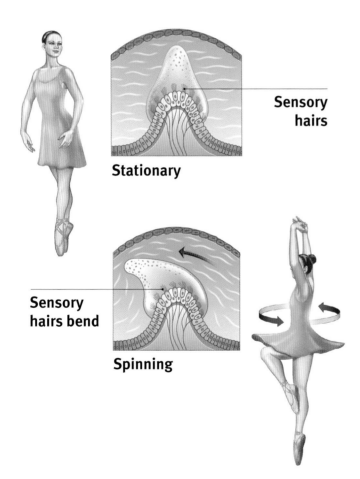

Sensory hairs

Stationary

Sensory hairs bend

Spinning

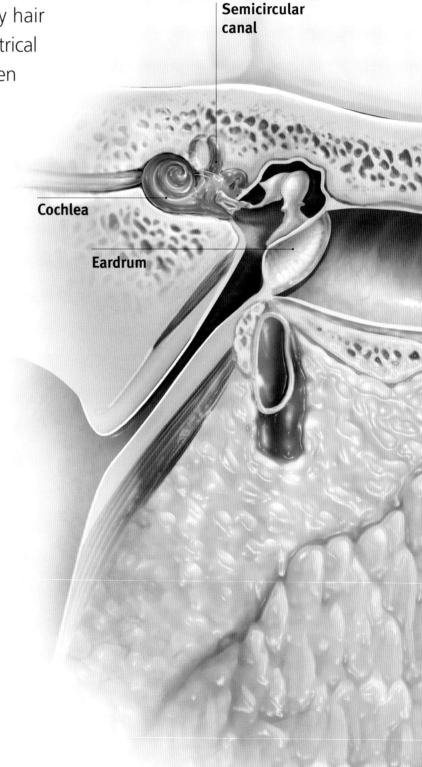

Semicircular canal

Cochlea

Eardrum

Your ears help you balance. Semicircular canals hold a fluid that moves with your body. Tiny hairs, called balance receptors, sense movement and tell the brain where your head is positioned.

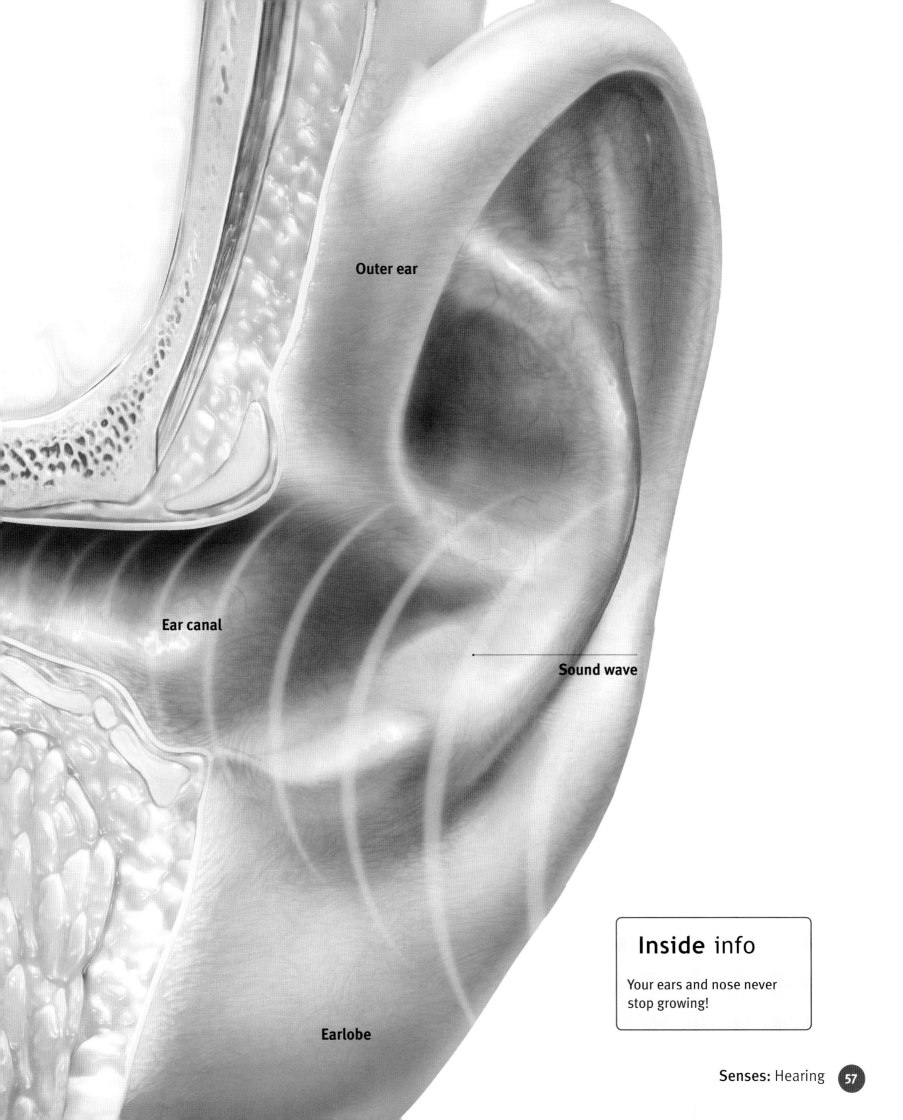

Outer ear

Ear canal

Sound wave

Earlobe

Inside info

Your ears and nose never stop growing!

TASTE

The surface of your tongue is covered with about 10,000 taste buds. Inside these taste buds are taste-detecting nerve cells. When food enters your mouth, it is dissolved by saliva and then chemicals are released. The receptors sense the chemicals and send signals to the brain. These receptors also act as a natural warning system for the body and tell us if something is dangerous by sensing a bitter taste.

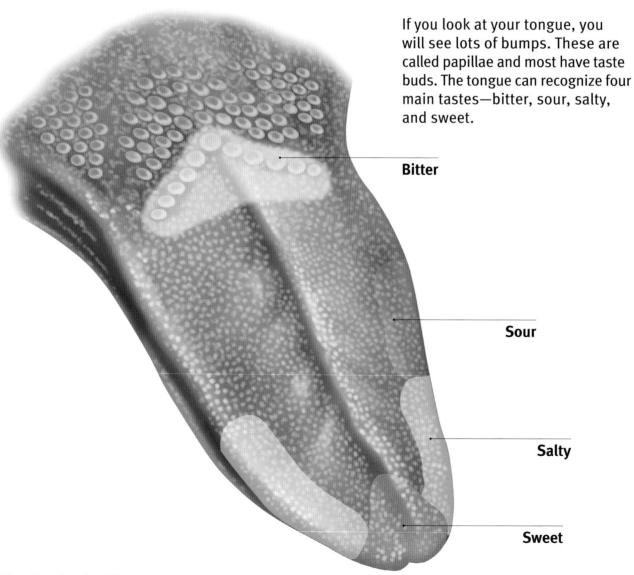

If you look at your tongue, you will see lots of bumps. These are called papillae and most have taste buds. The tongue can recognize four main tastes—bitter, sour, salty, and sweet.

Bitter

Sour

Salty

Sweet

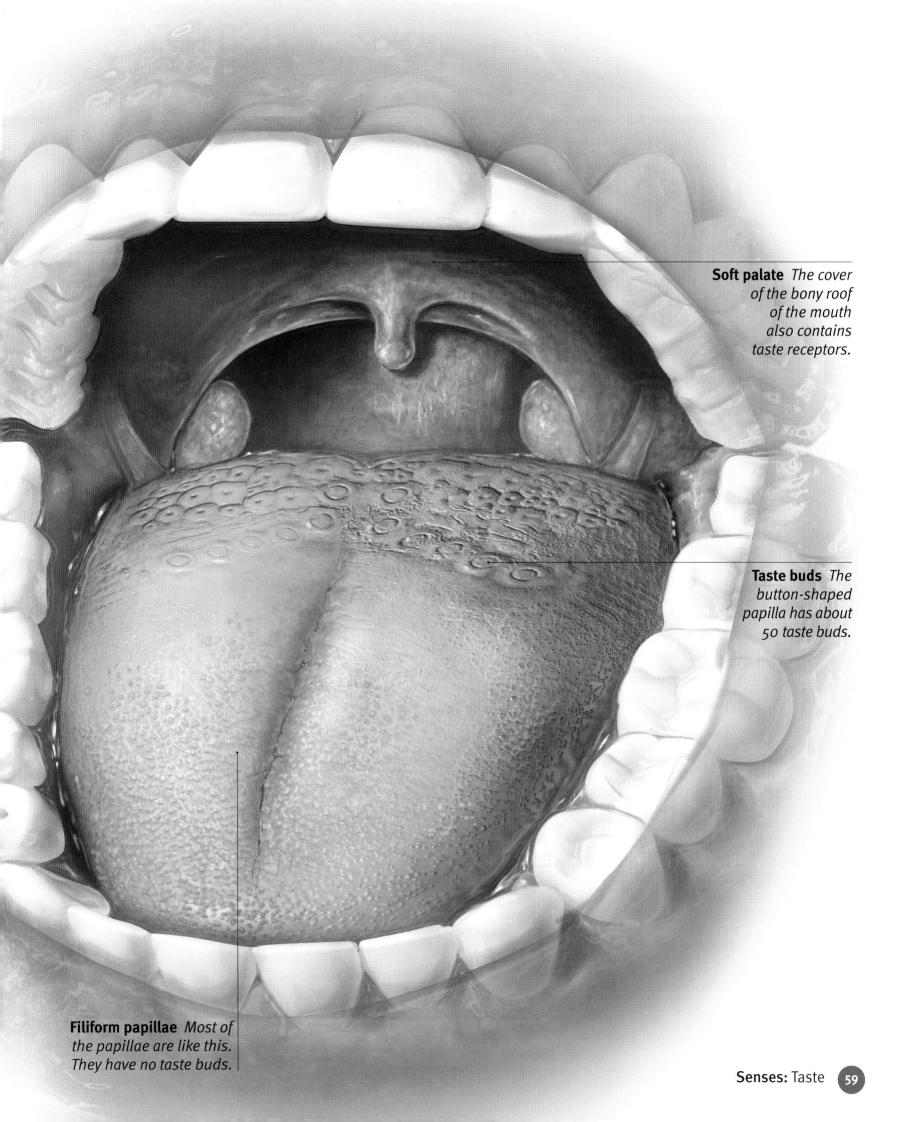

Soft palate *The cover of the bony roof of the mouth also contains taste receptors.*

Taste buds *The button-shaped papilla has about 50 taste buds.*

Filiform papillae *Most of the papillae are like this. They have no taste buds.*

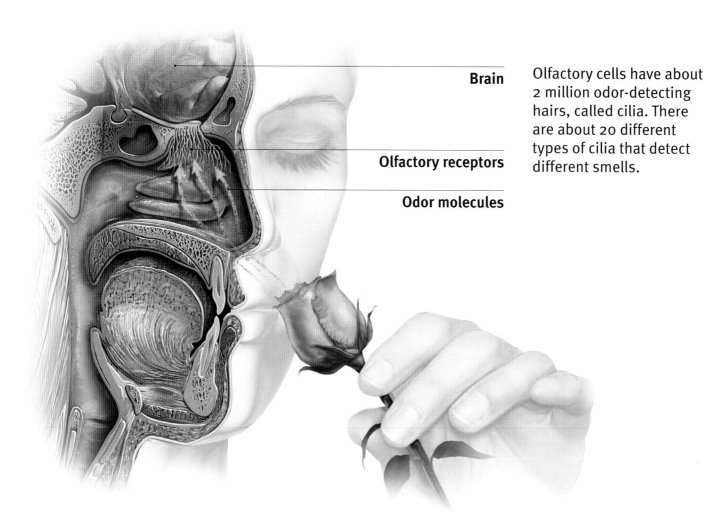

Brain

Olfactory receptors

Odor molecules

Olfactory cells have about 2 million odor-detecting hairs, called cilia. There are about 20 different types of cilia that detect different smells.

SMELL

Taste and smell work together so that you can fully experience flavor. When you have a head cold, your sense of smell does not work very well and it becomes hard to taste food. Smelling is done by a group of olfactory, or odor, receptors found in the upper part of the nose. When odor molecules enter your nose, the receptors send signals to the brain, which can then figure out what it is you are smelling.

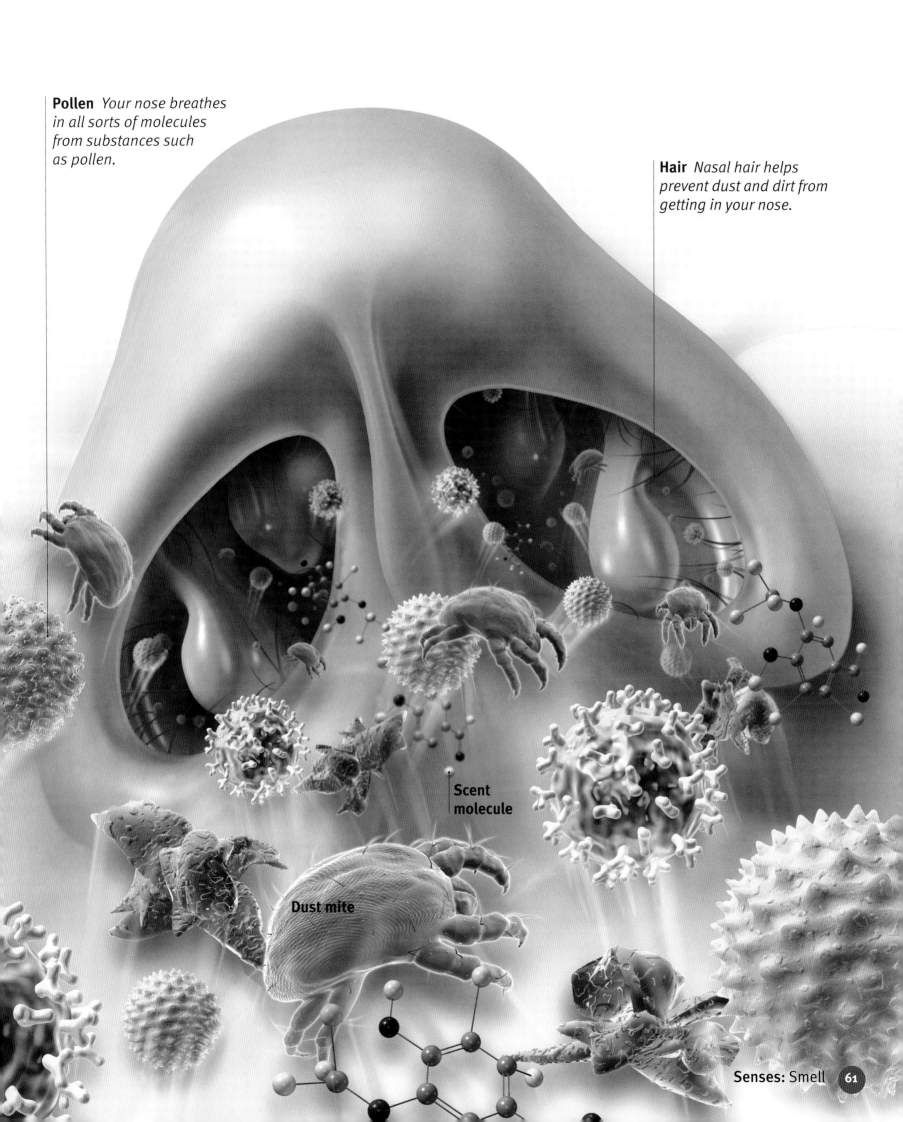

Pollen *Your nose breathes in all sorts of molecules from substances such as pollen.*

Hair *Nasal hair helps prevent dust and dirt from getting in your nose.*

Scent molecule

Dust mite

MUSCLES

Most of your body is made up of skeletal muscles, which support your skeleton and allow you to move. These muscles are called voluntary muscles because you can control their movement. They are connected to your bones by tendons, which are like flexible cables. There are more than 600 skeletal muscles in different shapes and sizes.

Much of your movement comes from muscles at the back of your body, which move your head, neck, spine, and arms. Muscles in the back of your thighs and legs allow you to walk, run, and jump.

Frontalis *Covers the front of your skull; it wrinkles your forehead when you frown.*

Orbicularis oris *This round muscle is sometimes called the "kissing muscle" because it closes and puckers the lips.*

Pectoralis major *You use this large chest muscle to push, throw, and climb.*

Biceps brachii *Draws your forearm forward.*

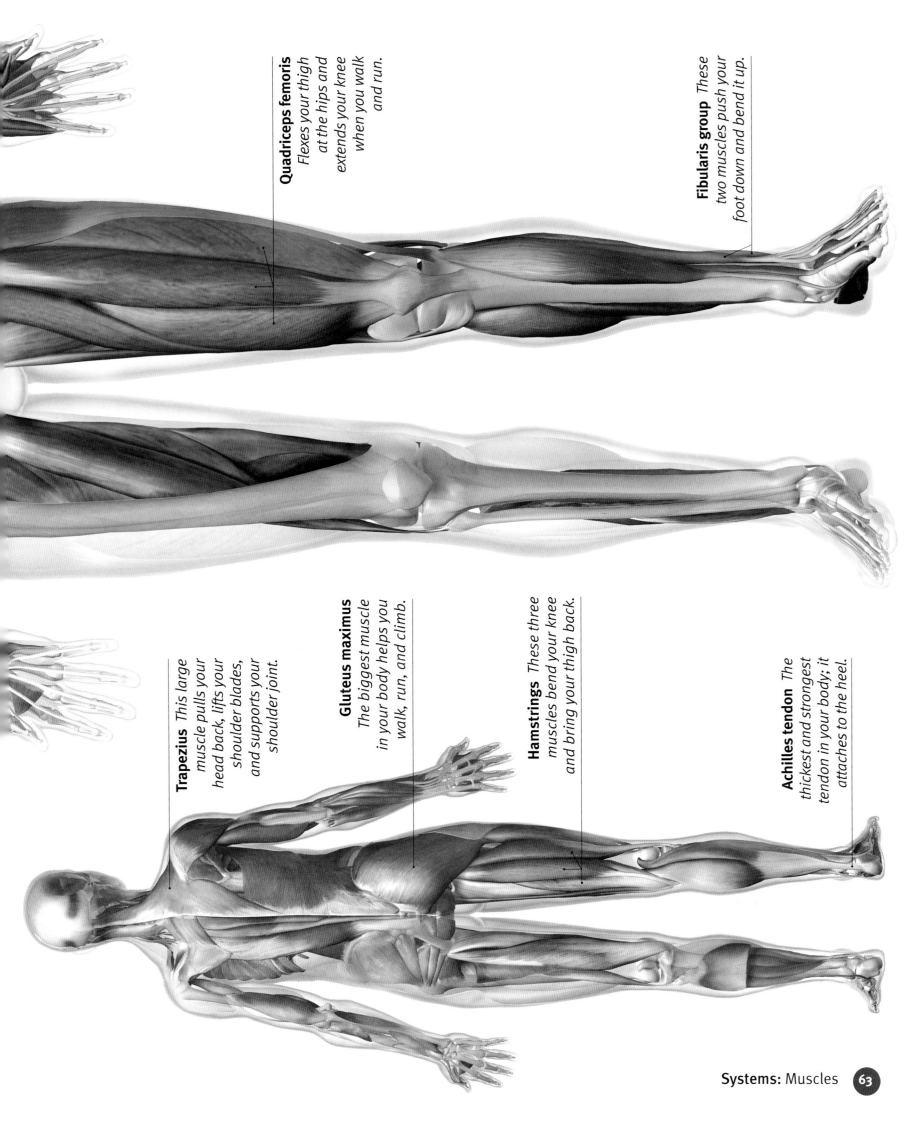

Quadriceps femoris *Flexes your thigh at the hips and extends your knee when you walk and run.*

Fibularis group *These two muscles push your foot down and bend it up.*

Trapezius *This large muscle pulls your head back, lifts your shoulder blades, and supports your shoulder joint.*

Gluteus maximus *The biggest muscle in your body helps you walk, run, and climb.*

Hamstrings *These three muscles bend your knee and bring your thigh back.*

Achilles tendon *The thickest and strongest tendon in your body; it attaches to the heel.*

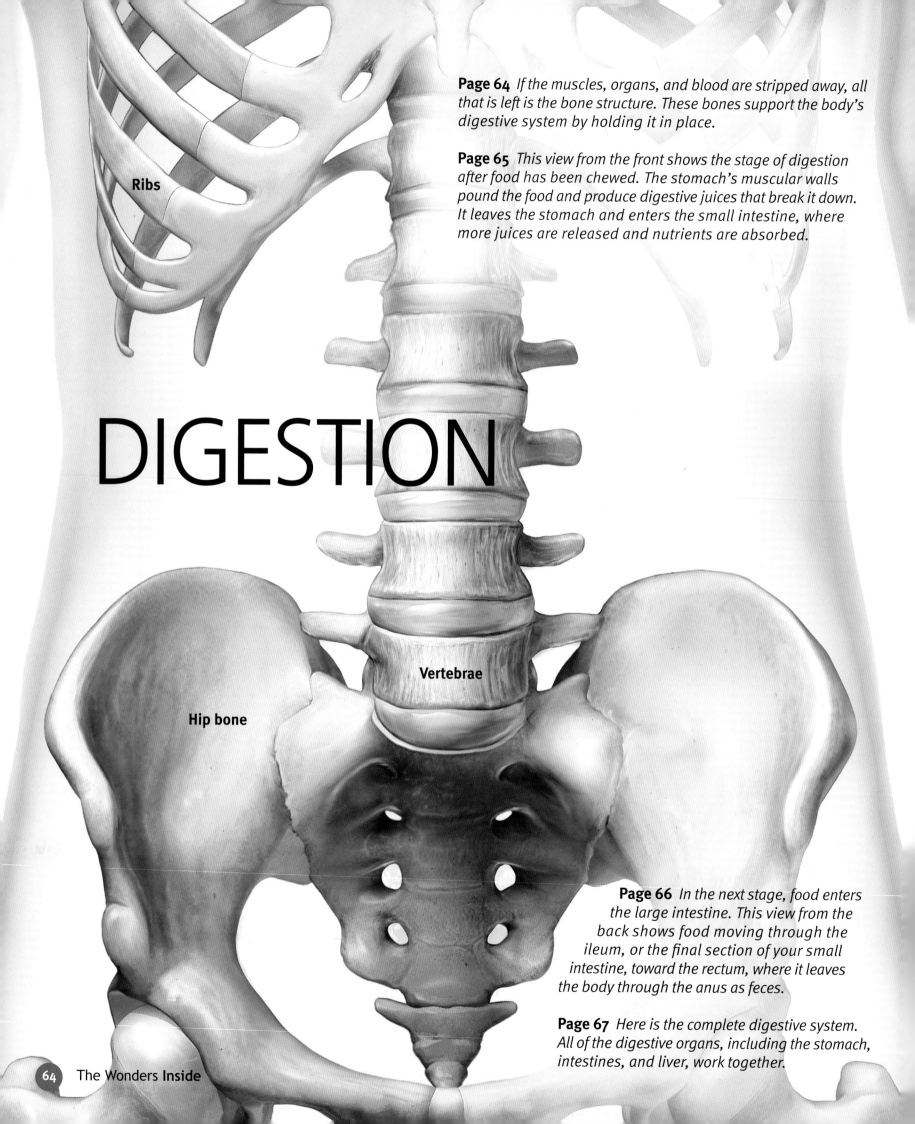

Ribs

Page 64 *If the muscles, organs, and blood are stripped away, all that is left is the bone structure. These bones support the body's digestive system by holding it in place.*

Page 65 *This view from the front shows the stage of digestion after food has been chewed. The stomach's muscular walls pound the food and produce digestive juices that break it down. It leaves the stomach and enters the small intestine, where more juices are released and nutrients are absorbed.*

DIGESTION

Vertebrae

Hip bone

Page 66 *In the next stage, food enters the large intestine. This view from the back shows food moving through the ileum, or the final section of your small intestine, toward the rectum, where it leaves the body through the anus as feces.*

Page 67 *Here is the complete digestive system. All of the digestive organs, including the stomach, intestines, and liver, work together.*

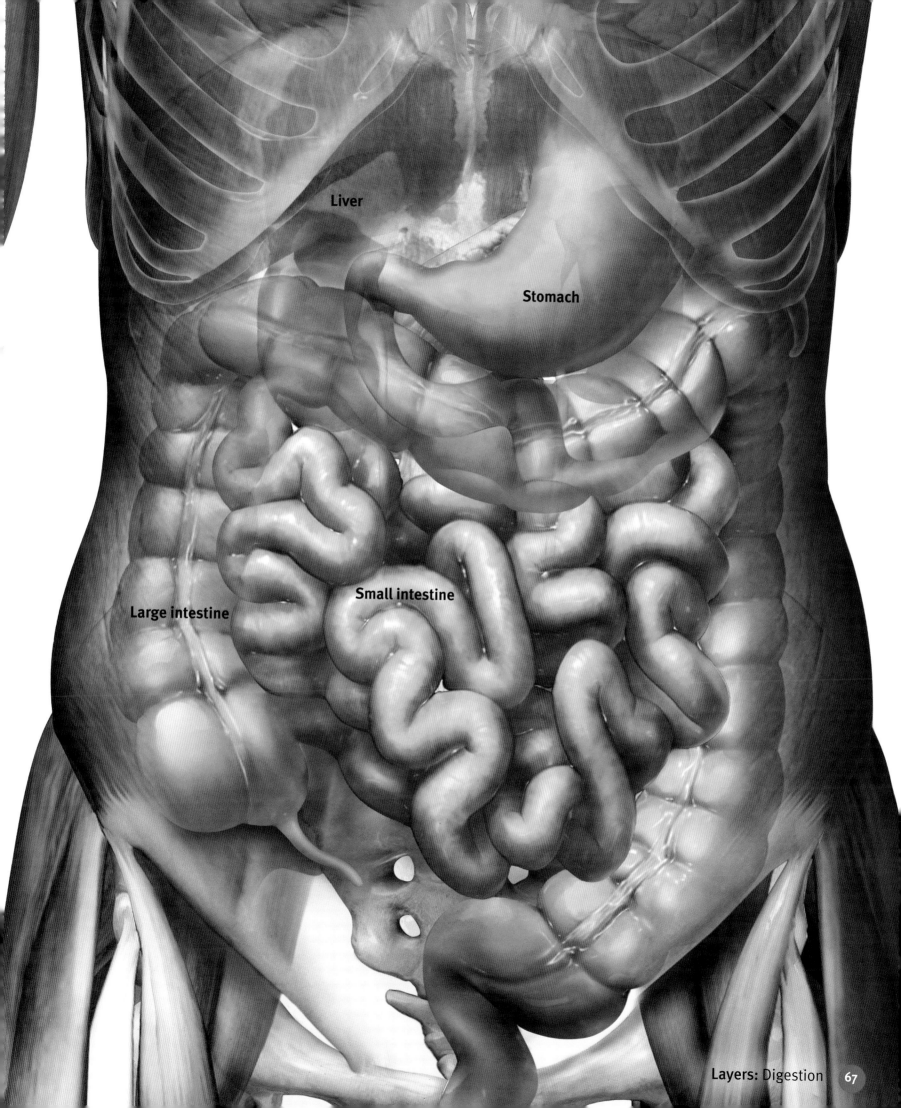

Liver

Stomach

Small intestine

Large intestine

SKELETON

Your skeleton is made up of more than 200 bones and has two main parts. One part of your skeleton includes your skull, spinal column, ribs, and breastbone. The other part includes the bones in your arms, legs, and near your chest and waist, and helps your body to move. Without your skeleton, your body would have no shape.

Inside info

You have the same number of bones in your neck as a giraffe. Its vertebrae are just a lot longer.

Frontal bone *Forms the front of the skull and the upper eye sockets.*

Ear bones *The middle ear contains the smallest bones in your body.*

Sternum
The breastbone connects the ribs and shoulders.

Ribs *Protect your heart and lungs.*

Spine *Your spine has 33 backbones, or vertebrae.*

Coxal bone *Also called the hip bone; it forms most of the pelvis.*

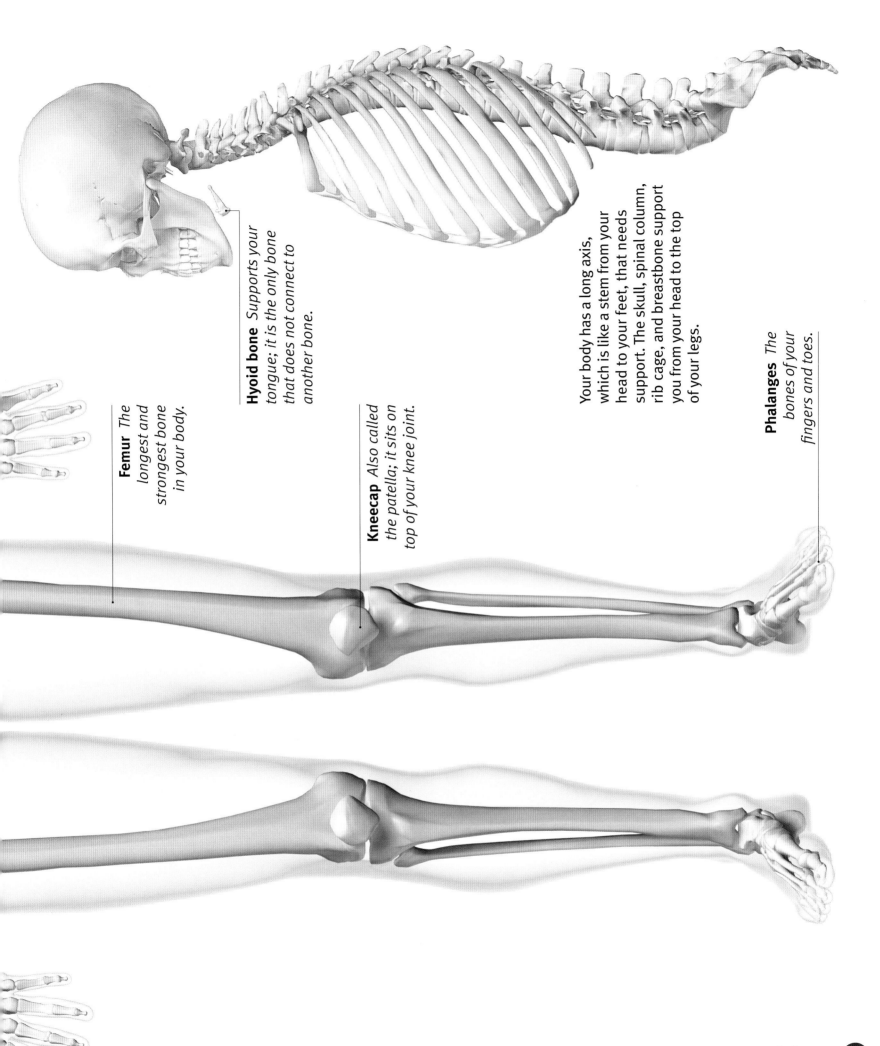

Hyoid bone *Supports your tongue; it is the only bone that does not connect to another bone.*

Femur *The longest and strongest bone in your body.*

Kneecap *Also called the patella; it sits on top of your knee joint.*

Your body has a long axis, which is like a stem from your head to your feet, that needs support. The skull, spinal column, rib cage, and breastbone support you from your head to the top of your legs.

Phalanges *The bones of your fingers and toes.*

Frontal sinus
In your forehead, above your eyes.

Ethmoidal sinus
Between your nose and eyes.

Sphenoidal sinus
Behind your nose and eyes.

Maxillary sinus
In your upper jaw, close to your cheekbones.

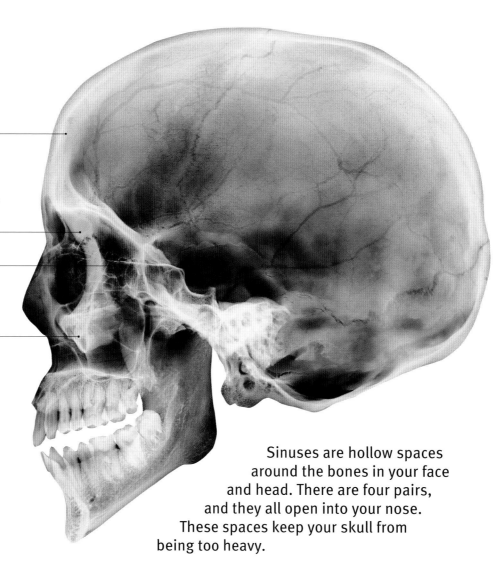

Frontal bone *The hard, thick bone of your forehead helps protect your brain.*

Sinuses are hollow spaces around the bones in your face and head. There are four pairs, and they all open into your nose. These spaces keep your skull from being too heavy.

THE SKULL

Nasal bone *Two bones are paired to make the upper part of the bridge of your nose.*

Your skull protects your brain and connects with muscles in your face and neck. It consists of 29 bones—14 of these are from your face and hold your eyes in place to give your face its shape. The other bones form the cranium, which is your forehead and the bones at the back of your head. Most of the bones in your face come in pairs, so one side of your face mirrors the other.

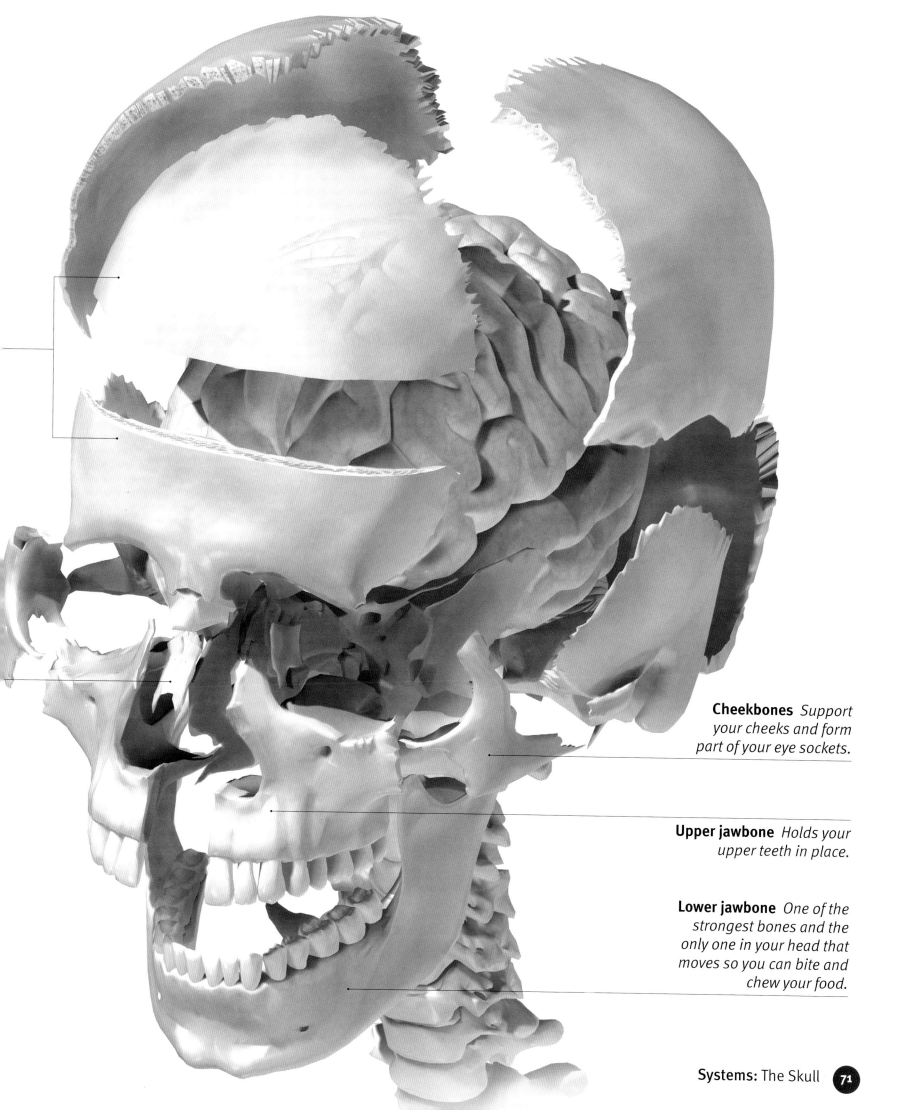

Cheekbones *Support your cheeks and form part of your eye sockets.*

Upper jawbone *Holds your upper teeth in place.*

Lower jawbone *One of the strongest bones and the only one in your head that moves so you can bite and chew your food.*

BONES

Bones have to be strong and hard to support our bodies and protect soft body parts. The smooth outer part of a bone is made from heavy, thick bone tissue and the inner layer is made of light, spongy bone tissue. There are cavities inside the spongy tissue that are filled with bone marrow. Some bones have red marrow, which makes new blood cells.

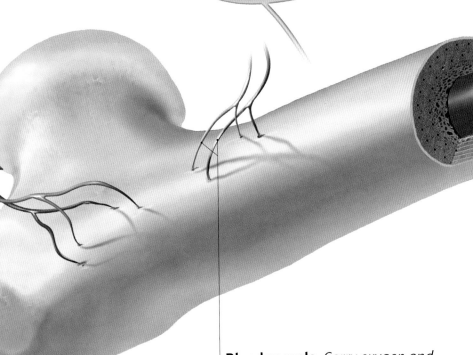

Nerve *Carries signals to other parts of the bone.*

Bone marrow
This yellow marrow stores fat.

Blood vessels *Carry oxygen and nutrients to bone and take away unwanted waste.*

Inside info

Bones are living things! A bone's tough exterior is made of strong fibers and minerals, as well as living cells with blood and nerves. But if you break a bone, it can take three months to heal.

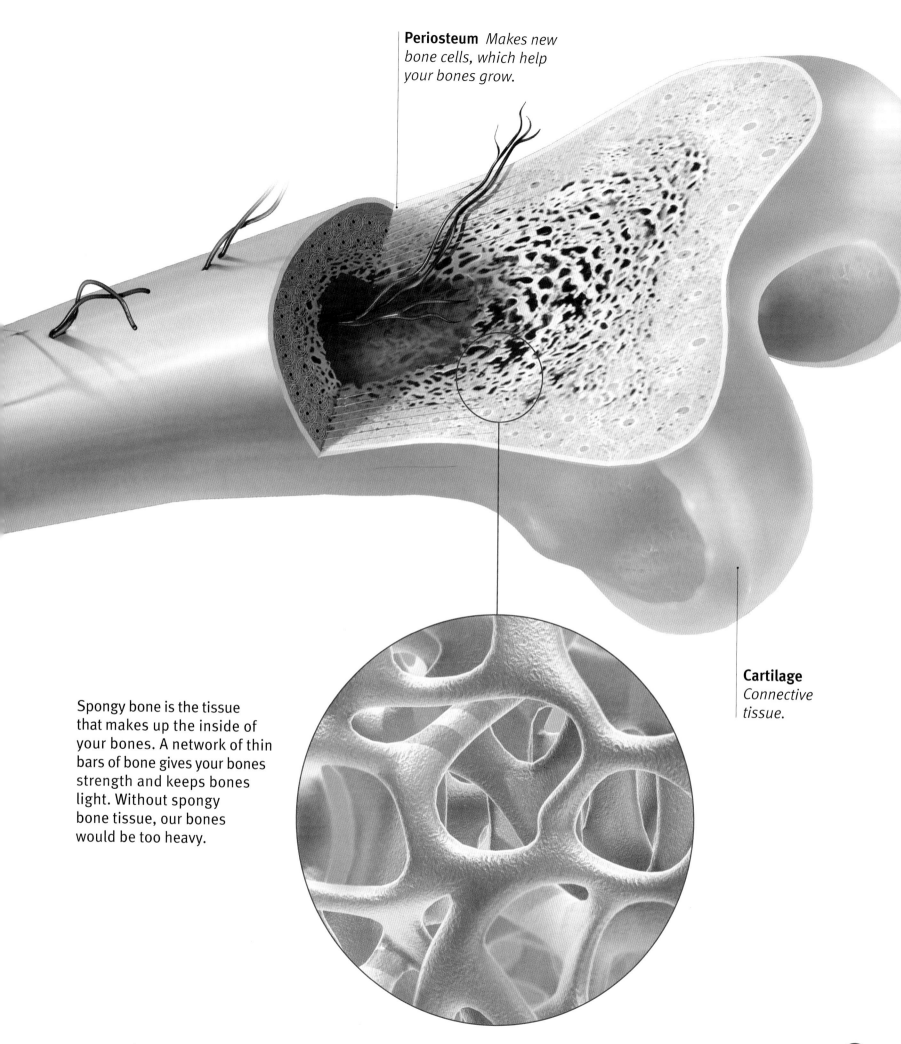

Periosteum *Makes new bone cells, which help your bones grow.*

Cartilage *Connective tissue.*

Spongy bone is the tissue that makes up the inside of your bones. A network of thin bars of bone gives your bones strength and keeps bones light. Without spongy bone tissue, our bones would be too heavy.

CIRCULATORY SYSTEM

Your heart pumps blood around your body in blood vessels called arteries, capillaries, and veins. Blood vessels are like roads—they take your blood wherever it needs to go. Because your blood has to make the right deliveries to trillions of cells, it picks things up and drops things off on the way around your body. For example, at the lungs it stops for fresh oxygen while it drops off carbon dioxide.

Inside info

Most people have more than a gallon of blood going around their body. It only takes 20 seconds for a blood cell to make a delivery and return to your heart.

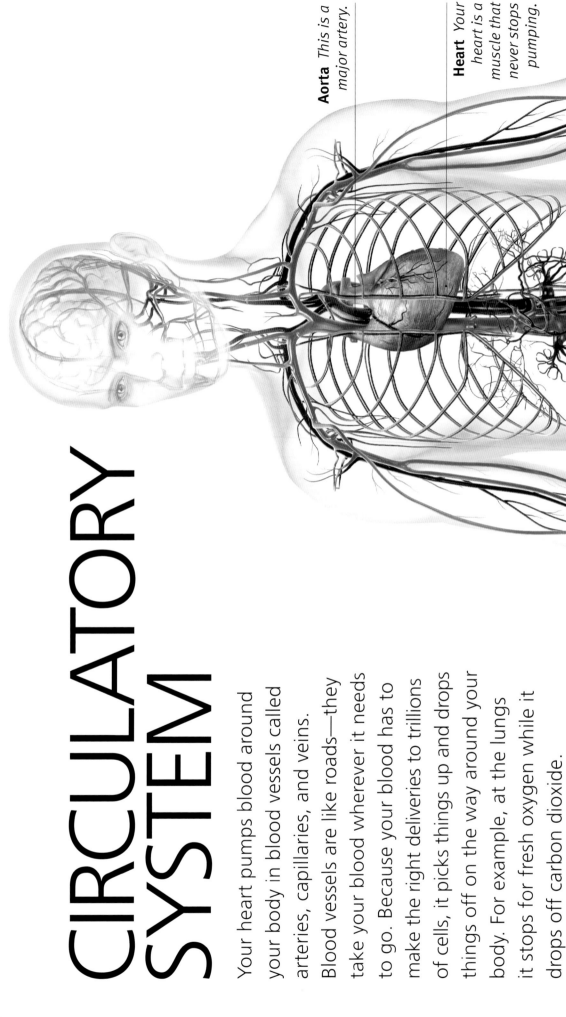

Aorta *This is a major artery.*

Heart *Your heart is a muscle that never stops pumping.*

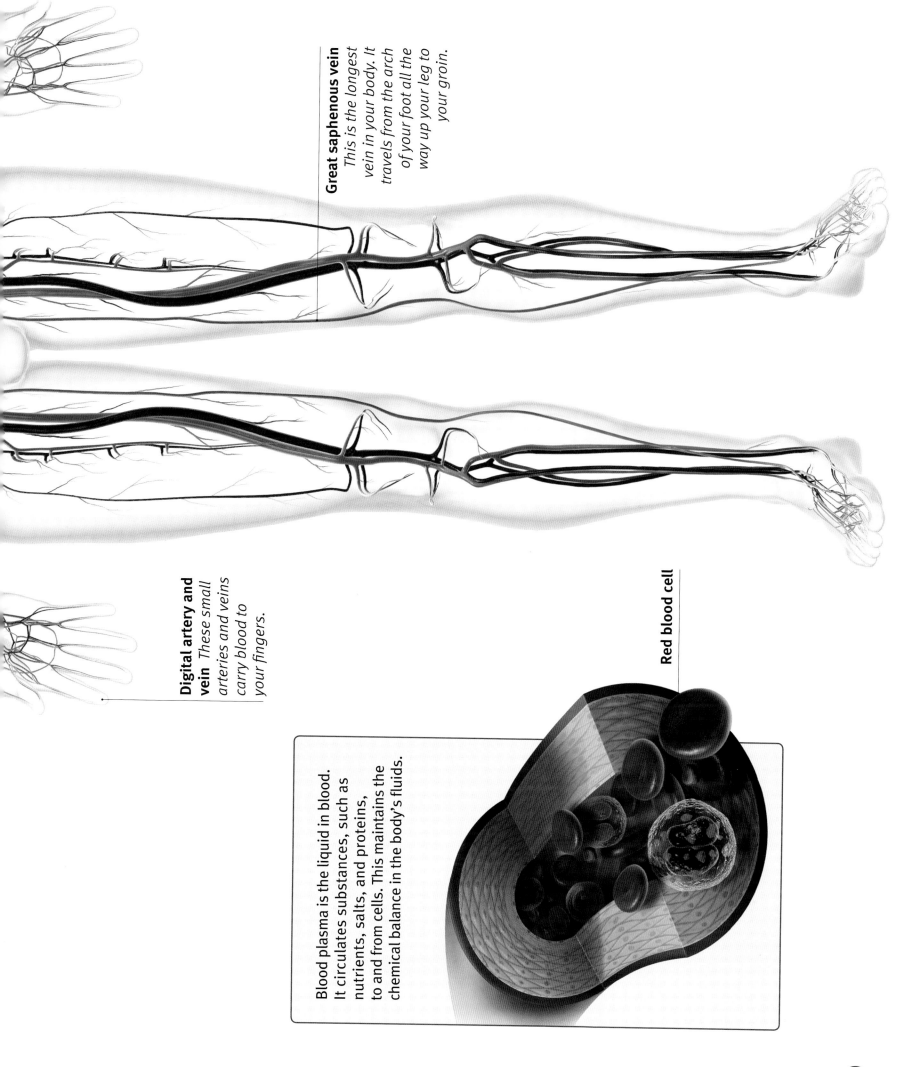

Great saphenous vein *This is the longest vein in your body. It travels from the arch of your foot all the way up your leg to your groin.*

Digital artery and vein *These small arteries and veins carry blood to your fingers.*

Red blood cell

Blood plasma is the liquid in blood. It circulates substances, such as nutrients, salts, and proteins, to and from cells. This maintains the chemical balance in the body's fluids.

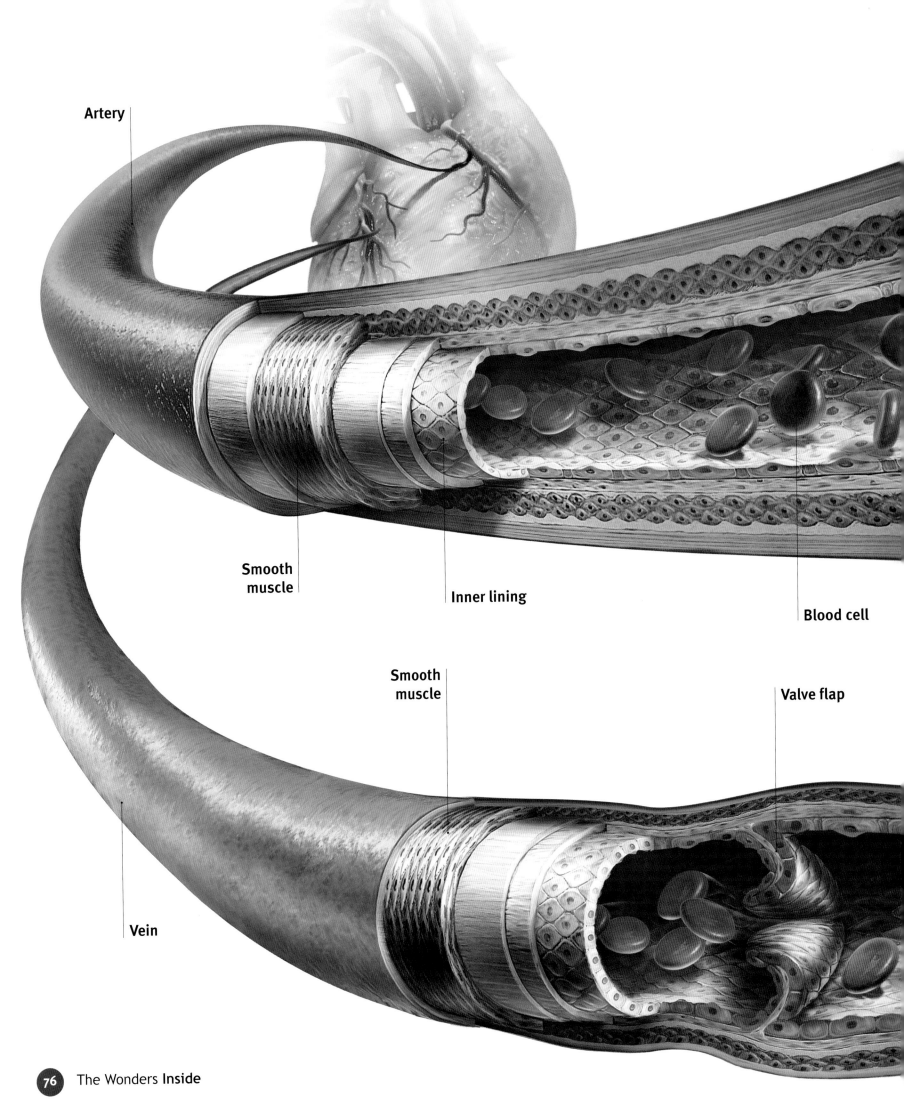

Artery

Smooth
muscle

Inner lining

Blood cell

Smooth
muscle

Valve flap

Vein

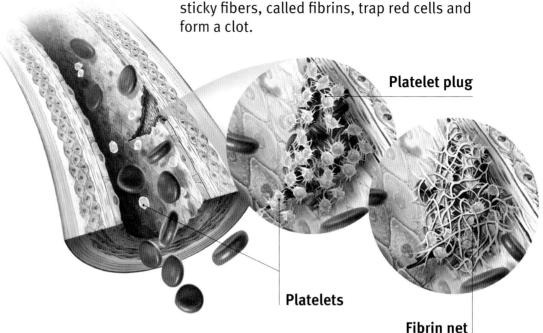

When a small vessel is damaged, platelets and sticky fibers, called fibrins, trap red cells and form a clot.

Platelet plug

Platelets

Fibrin net

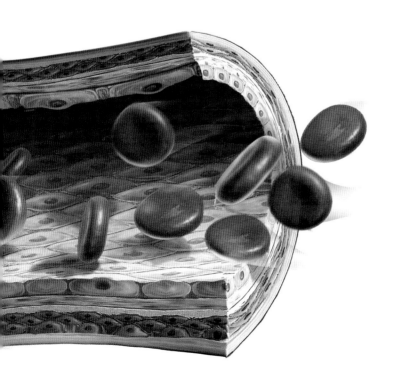

BLOOD VESSELS

There are two main types of blood vessels: arteries and veins. Arteries have thick, tough, stretchy walls and carry blood away from your heart. Veins carry blood back to your heart. Veins contain valves, which control the blood flow and make sure it does not flow backward when it is traveling back. Other types of blood vessels are arterioles, capillaries, and venules. They all help transport blood around the body and maintain your circulation.

NERVOUS SYSTEM

Every part of your body is connected to your brain by nerves. Your brain is the control center of the nervous system. Tens of millions of nerve cells called neurons send signals that let your brain know what is happening inside and outside your body. The central nervous system reads the signals and sends back more signals that tell your body what to do.

Brain

Cranial nerves

Spinal cord *The spinal cord is a busy highway that carries signals to and from your brain.*

Median nerve *This works with the muscles in your lower arm, wrist, and fingers.*

Inside info

Adults have about 47 miles of nerves in their bodies.

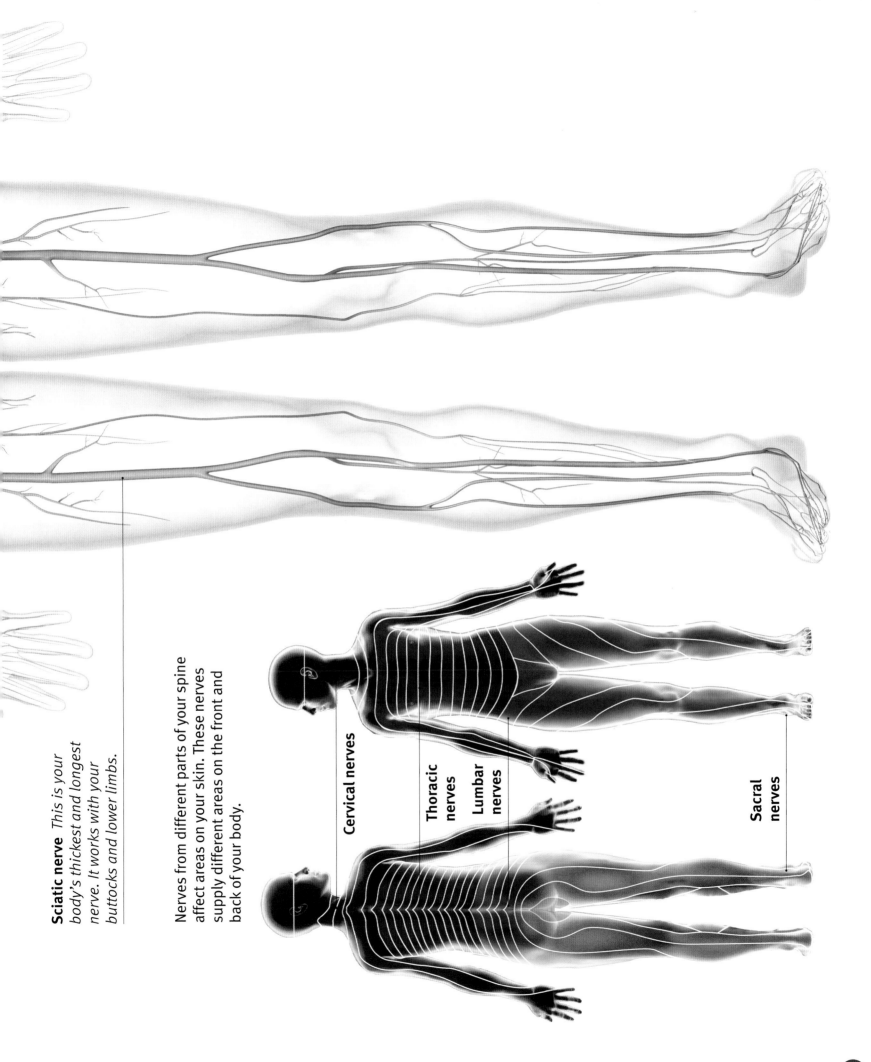

Sciatic nerve *This is your body's thickest and longest nerve. It works with your buttocks and lower limbs.*

Nerves from different parts of your spine affect areas on your skin. These nerves supply different areas on the front and back of your body.

Cervical nerves

Thoracic nerves

Lumbar nerves

Sacral nerves

NERVES

Each nerve in your body is made of thousands of nerve cells, called neurons. These long cells can send a nerve message as fast as 300 feet per second. The message travels along the neuron's "arm," or axon, and across tiny gaps to other nerve cells—these gaps are called synapses. Then the dendrites receive the message and it is passed on until it reaches its destination.

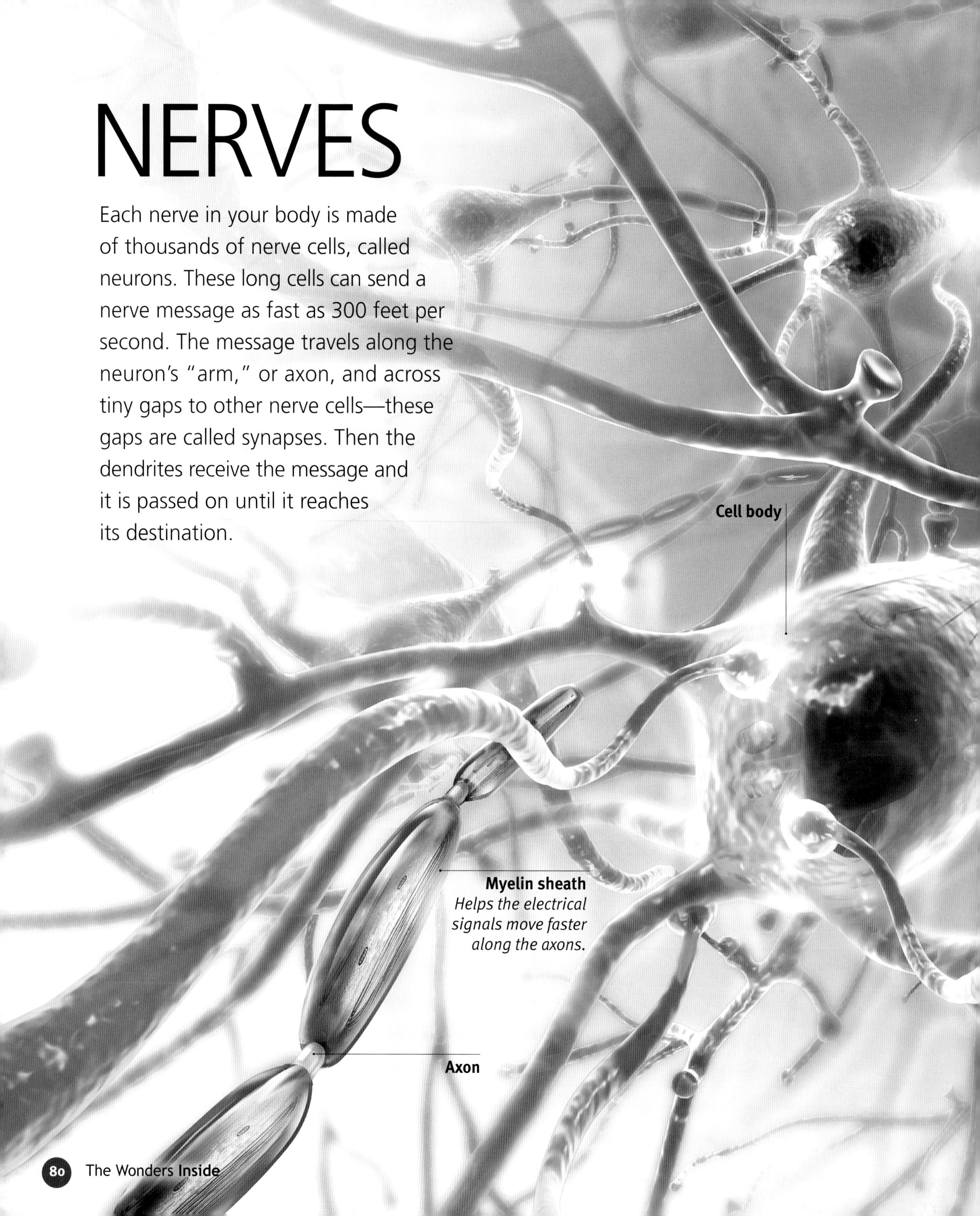

Cell body

Myelin sheath
Helps the electrical signals move faster along the axons.

Axon

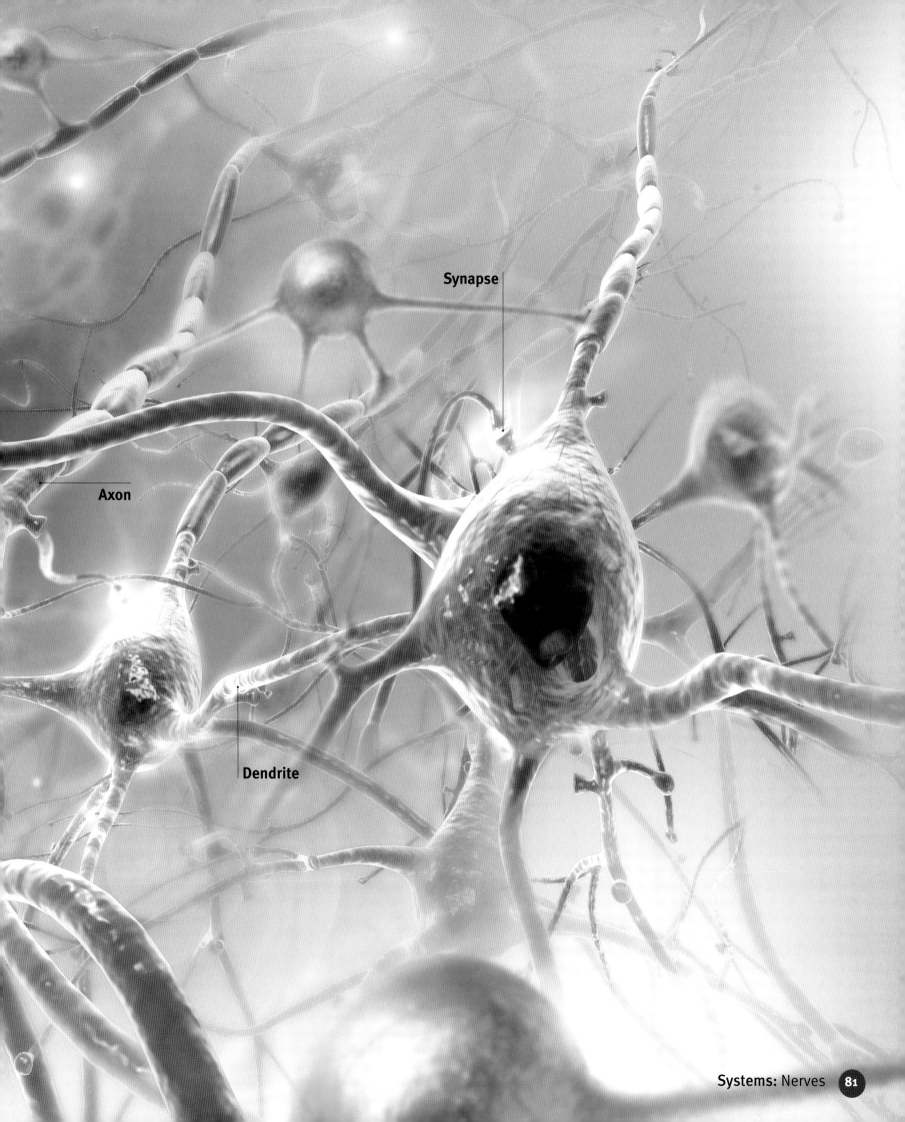

Synapse

Axon

Dendrite

ENDOCRINE SYSTEM

The endocrine system produces hormones, which are your body's chemical messengers. Some hormones are made by your endocrine glands, and others form in body tissue in organs such as your stomach and your heart. Glands also create other substances for your body to use, such as digestive juices, sweat, saliva, and tears. Hormones work with your nervous system to control and adjust your body. They help you digest your food, keep your body temperature constant, and control how your body grows. They can make you feel hungry, thirsty, or tired. There are 30 different hormones and they all have different jobs.

Hypothalamus
Makes more hormones than any other gland. It also controls most hormones.

Pituitary gland
Makes hormones and stores the ones made by the hypothalamus.

Thyroid gland
Controls your energy levels.

Thymus gland *Makes a hormone that affects the body's defenses.*

Heart *A hormone from the heart helps adjust blood pressure.*

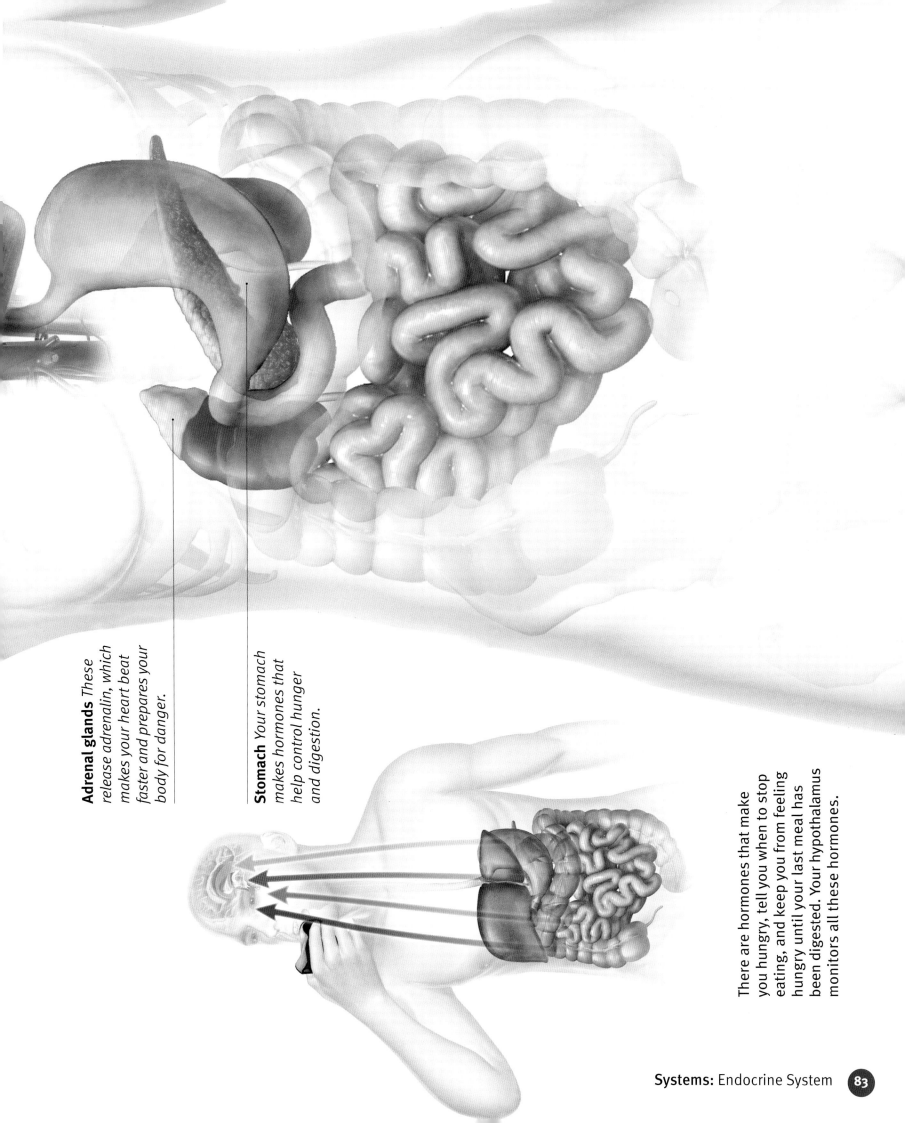

Adrenal glands *These release adrenalin, which makes your heart beat faster and prepares your body for danger.*

Stomach *Your stomach makes hormones that help control hunger and digestion.*

There are hormones that make you hungry, tell you when to stop eating, and keep you from feeling hungry until your last meal has been digested. Your hypothalamus monitors all these hormones.

LYMPHATIC SYSTEM

Your lymphatic system is made up of lymphatic vessels, which work to protect your body from germs and infection. Your blood vessels leak a clear liquid called lymph, which contains water and other good things. The lymphatic vessels collect the lymph and return it to your bloodstream. Before they return it, tiny organs called lymph nodes work with other tissues and organs to make white blood cells that fight off germs.

Spleen *Cleans your blood and gets rid of germs.*

Red bone marrow *This is where white and red blood cells develop.*

Tonsils *You have four sets of tonsils that help fight infection.*

Axillary nodes *There are 20 to 30 lymph nodes around your armpits.*

Appendix *This lymphatic organ can gather too many germs and become infected.*

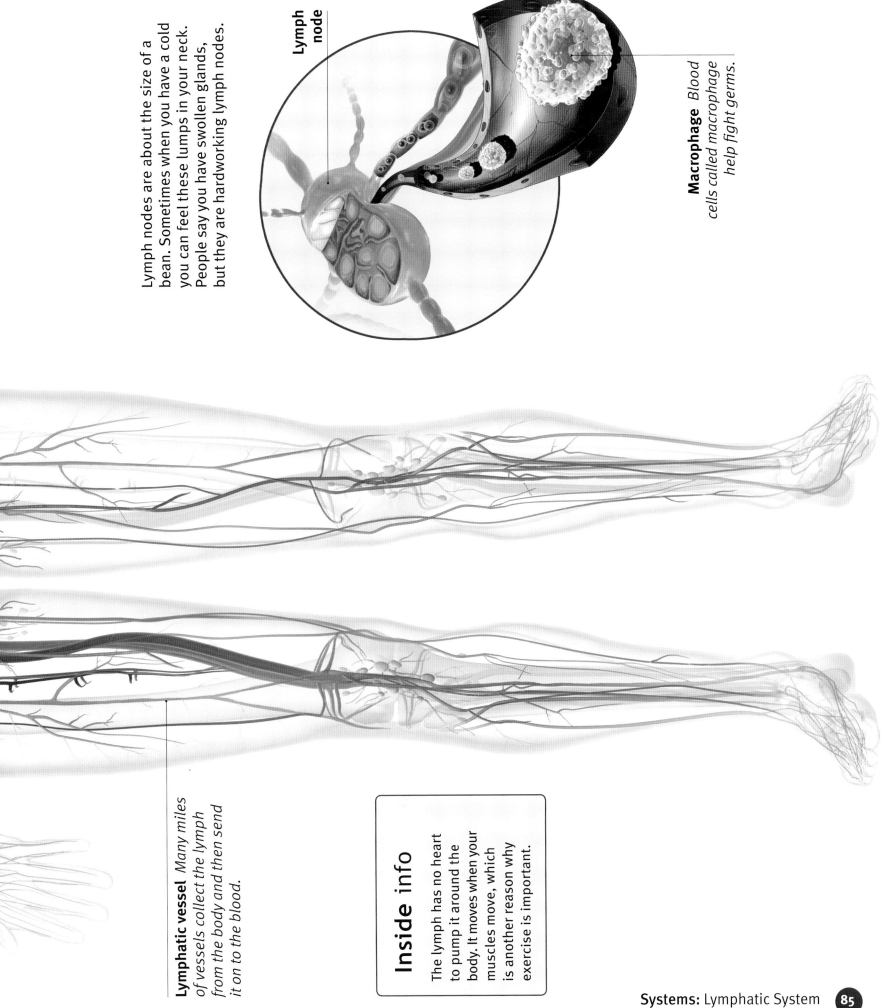

Lymph node

Lymph nodes are about the size of a bean. Sometimes when you have a cold you can feel these lumps in your neck. People say you have swollen glands, but they are hardworking lymph nodes.

Macrophage *Blood cells called macrophage help fight germs.*

Lymphatic vessel *Many miles of vessels collect the lymph from the body and then send it on to the blood.*

Inside info

The lymph has no heart to pump it around the body. It moves when your muscles move, which is another reason why exercise is important.

DEFENSES

Your body has a tough defense system and has many clever ways to keep germs out and fight them if they get inside your body. When harmful bacteria or viruses enter your body, it makes special proteins, called antibodies, to destroy them. Antibodies travel around your bloodstream to fight disease.

Hair follicles *Make a chemical called sebum, which stops bacteria from growing.*

Eyes *Tears contain a chemical that protects the eye.*

Mouth and throat *Saliva contains chemicals to fight germs.*

Skin *Most germs cannot get past your tough skin.*

Respiratory tract *Airways are covered in tiny hairs that trap anything dangerous.*

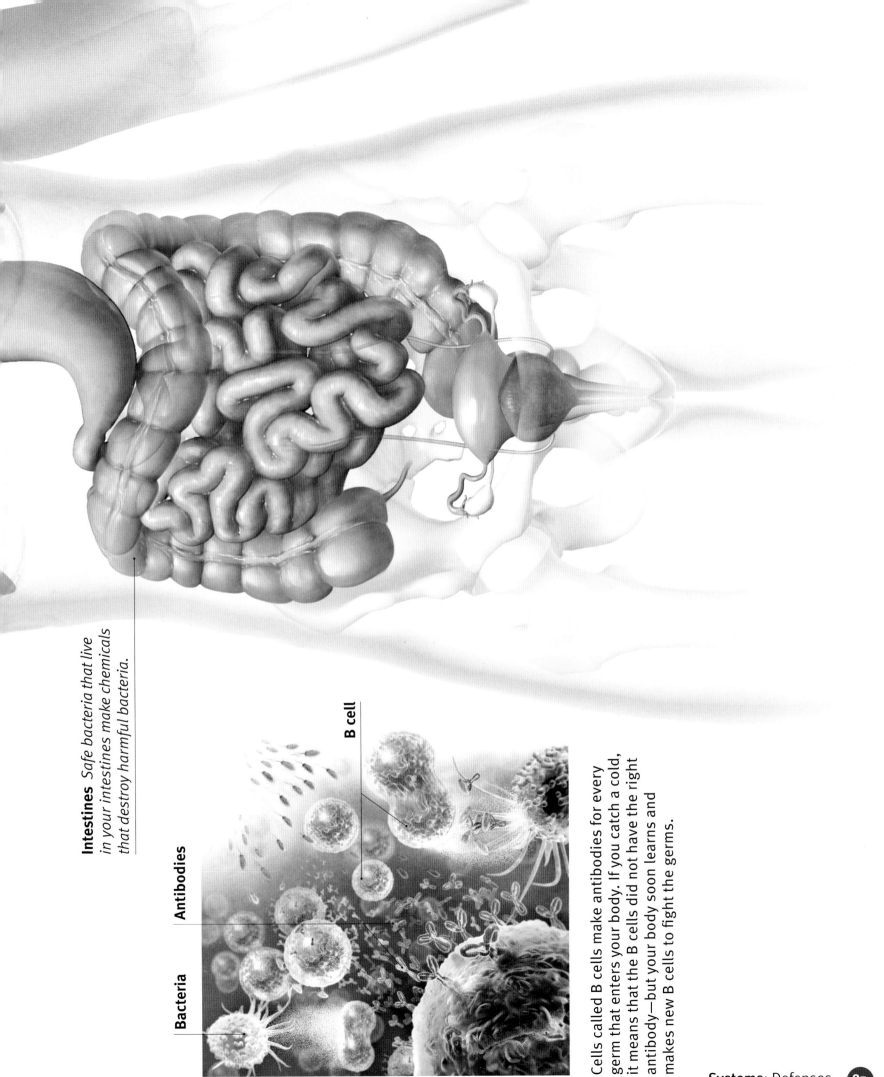

Intestines *Safe bacteria that live in your intestines make chemicals that destroy harmful bacteria.*

Bacteria

Antibodies

B cell

Cells called B cells make antibodies for every germ that enters your body. If you catch a cold, it means that the B cells did not have the right antibody—but your body soon learns and makes new B cells to fight the germs.

GLOSSARY

ANTIBODY
A chemical made by special blood cells to help fight germs. Antibodies are part of the body's defense system, which helps prevent disease.

ARTERY
A large blood vessel that carries blood full of fresh oxygen away from the heart and toward the parts of the body that need it.

BACTERIA
Small, one-celled organisms. Some bacteria are germs and can be harmful, but other bacteria help fight germs and keep the body healthy.

BLOOD CELLS
The two kinds of cells that make up the blood. Red blood cells carry oxygen to other cells and pick up carbon dioxide. White blood cells fight germs.

BLOOD VESSELS
Different-sized tubes that carry blood around the body as part of the circulation system. Arteries and veins are the main blood vessels but there are also capillaries, which connect them to each other.

CARBON DIOXIDE
A gas that is a waste product made by cells when they use energy. The blood carries carbon dioxide to the lungs to be exhaled.

CELL
The smallest living thing that can work by itself. All living things are made up of cells.

CENTRAL NERVOUS SYSTEM
The spinal cord and brain make up the central nervous system—they control everything the body does and feels.

CHROMOSOME
A tiny strand in the center of each cell. It carries genetic information inherited from the parents, such as eye color.

CIRCULATION
The movement of blood and other fluids as the heart pumps it around the body.

COLLAGEN
A flexible type of protein, which connects and supports tendons, cartilage, and skin.

COMPACT BONE
The hard, dense outer layer of bones that gives them strength and makes them smooth and white. Bones have an outer shell of compact bone with spongy bone inside.

DENDRITE
Short strands that branch off nerve cells. Dendrites carry and receive electrical signals to and from the nerve cell, or neuron.

DIAPHRAGM
A sheet of muscle found below the lungs, between the chest cavity and the abdomen. The diaphragm is the main muscle used to breathe.

DNA
The chemical that makes up the chromosomes and genes that are inherited from parents. DNA can only be seen with a microscope. It looks like a twisted ladder and is found in all body cells.

EMBRYO
A developing animal that is still in the womb. A human baby is called an embryo for the first eight weeks of its life.

ENDOCRINE SYSTEM
A network of glands that produces hormones. These give the body the chemicals it needs to perform different jobs.

FETUS
An unborn animal still in the womb. A human baby is called a fetus from eight weeks old until it is born.

GENE
A code that decides how the body will grow. Genes are inherited from parents and they determine things such as whether hair is straight or curly.

HYPOTHALAMUS

A part of the brain that controls hunger, thirst, tiredness, and emotions, such as anger. It also helps to keep the body temperature constant.

INVOLUNTARY MUSCLES

Muscles that move on their own. The heart is an involuntary muscle that beats all day and all night. Other involuntary muscles are found in places such as the eyes and stomach.

MEMBRANE

A thin cover that protects cells and organs in the same way skin protects the outside of the body.

NERVES

Bundles of nerve fibers that carry electrical signals between the body and the central nervous system. Many nerves connect to the brain through the spinal cord.

NEURON

A nerve cell that is part of the nervous system. Neurons send electrical messages from the brain to the body and back again.

NUCLEUS

The central part of almost every cell. The nucleus controls the cell's growth.

NUTRIENTS

Substances that provide humans with energy. They are absorbed from food and drink.

ORGAN

A part of the body that does a particular job. The human body is made up of groups of organs that work together in organ systems. For example, the stomach and intestines are organs of the digestive system.

OXYGEN

A gas that the body breathes in. It is carried by the blood to all of the cells and organs in the body. The cells use it to make the energy the body needs to live.

PROTEINS

Nutrients used for building the human body. Every cell is made up of protein that helps to build and replace the tissues in the body.

PUBERTY

The stage when the body begins to develop and change from a child to an adult.

SENSORY RECEPTORS

Sensory receptors allow humans to hear, see, taste, smell, touch, and balance.

SPONGY BONE

Bone that has many hollow spaces, like a honeycomb. Spongy bone is found inside compact bone.

TISSUE

A mass of cells that join with other cells. There are four different types of tissue in the body that have different functions.

VEIN

A hollow tube called a blood vessel. Veins usually carry oxygen-poor blood back to the heart.

VENTRICLE

One of two lower chambers in the heart from which blood is pumped to the lungs and to the rest of the body.

VERTEBRAE

The 33 bones that make up the backbone, or spine.

VOLUNTARY MUSCLES

Muscles that can move whenever the body instructs them. Voluntary muscles are used to perform activities such as running, jumping, lifting objects, and playing instruments.

INDEX

A
Achilles tendon 63
adrenal glands 83
amygdala 25
antibodies 84, 88
aorta 26, 75
appendix 84
arches, of foot 45
arms 32–33
arteries 9, 76–77, 88
atria 26, 28, 31

B
bacteria 86, 87, 88
balance 56
blood, circulation 31, 74–75, 88
blood cells 85, 88
  red 75, 76, 77
blood clots 16, 77
blood vessels *see* arteries; veins
bone marrow 72
  red 85
bones 9, 69, 72–73
  cheek 71
  compact 88
  ear 69
  frontal 71
  jaw 71
  nasal 71
  spongy tissue 73
brain 8, 22–23
  control center 79
  emotions 46–47
brain stem 23

C
calcaneus 44
capillaries 88
carbon dioxide 88
carpals 32
cartilage 73
cells 10–11, 88
cerebellum 23
cerebral cortex 23
cheekbones 71
chest 36–39

choroid 53
chromosomes 88
cilia 60
cingulate gyrus 25
circulation 31, 74–75, 88
cochlea 56
collagen 88
consciousness 23
cornea 50, 53, 55
cranial nerves 46, 79
cranium 70

D
dendrites 81, 88
dermis 49
diaphragm 88
digestion 64–67, 83
DNA 88

E
ears 56–57, 69
embryos 40, 88
emotions 24–25
endocrine system 82–83, 88
epidermis 19, 48, 49
eyes 50–53, 86
  sight 54–55

F
feet 44–45
femur 43, 69
fetus 40, 88
fibula 43
fingerprints 40
fingers 32
fingertips 48
flat feet 45
frontal bone 71
funny bone 32

G
genes 88
gluteus maximus 63
goosebumps 18
great saphenous vein 75

H
hair 20–21
  nasal 61
hair follicles 18, 21, 49, 86
hamstrings 63
head 12–15
hearing 56–57
heart 8, 26–29, 75, 83
  cardiac cycle 31
hip bones 64, 68
hippocampus 25
hormones 83
humerus 33
hunches 24
hyoid bone 69
hypothalamus 25, 82, 83, 88

I
ileum 66
inflammation 16
intestines 8, 65–67, 87
involuntary muscles 89
iris 50, 55

J
jawbone 71

K
keratin 20
kidneys 34–35
kneecaps 43, 69

L
legs 42–43
lens, of eye 50, 55
ligaments 43
liver 67
lungs 8, 37, 39, 75
lymph 84
lymphatic system 84–85
lymph nodes 84

M
macrophage 85
medulla oblongata 23

membranes 89
memory 24
metacarpals 32
metatarsals 44
mouth 86
muscles 9, 62–63, 85
  eye 54
  face 15
  involuntary 89
myelin sheath 80

N
nails 20
nerve endings 49
nerves 18, 79, 80–81, 89
nervous system 78–79, 88
neurons 80, 89
nose 57, 60–61, 71
nucleus 89

O
olfactory cells 60
optic nerve 50, 54

P
papillae 58, 59
pectoralis major 36
periosteum 73
phalanges 32, 44, 69
pituitary gland 83
placenta 40
prefrontal cortex 24
puberty 41
pupil 50, 55

R
radius 32
rectum 66
reproduction 40–41
respiratory tract 86
retina 52, 54, 55
ribs 37–38, 69

S
scabs 16
scapula 33

sciatic nerve 79
sclera 51, 53, 55
senses 46–47
sight 54–55
sinuses 70
skeleton 68–69
skin 18–19, 86
skull 12, 22, 70–71
smell 60–61
soft palate 59
spinal cord 23, 64, 69, 79
spleen 85
sternum 69
stomach 8, 65, 67, 83
sweat glands 18
synapses 80
synovial fluid 43

T
tarsals 43, 44
taste 58–59, 60
taste buds 58, 59
thalamus 25
thighbone 43
thymus 83
thyroid 83
tibia 43
tibialis anterior 43
tickling 46
tissue repair 16–17
toes 43
tongue 58–59
tonsils 85
touch 48–49
trapezius 63

U
ulna 32
umbilical cord 40, 41
urethra 35
urine 35
uterus 40

V
vagina 40
veins 9, 76–77, 88
ventricles 27, 29, 31
vertebrae 69

CREDITS

The publisher thanks Lachlan McLaine, Jen Taylor, and Shan Wolody for their contributions, and Jo Rudd for the index.

ILLUSTRATIONS
Illustrations by **Argosy Publishing**, www.argosypublishing.com, with the exception of some
ADDITIONAL ILLUSTRATIONS
Endpapers Sarah Norton
Susanna Addario 24 bottom left; **Peter Bull Art Studio** 43 top and 56 left; **Christer Eriksson** 54 bottom left

PHOTOGRAPH
70 Science Photo Library